Australian Police Tests

www.How2Become.com

As part of this product you have also received FREE access to online tests that will help you to become a Police Officer.

To gain access, simply go to:

www.MyPsychometricTests.co.uk

Get more products for passing any test at:

www.How2Become.com

Orders: Please contact How2Become Ltd, Suite 14, 50 Churchill Square Business Centre, Kings Hill, Kent ME19 4YU.

You can order through Amazon.co.uk under ISBN: 9781912370108, via the website www.How2Become.com or through Ingram.

ISBN: 9781912370108

First published in 2018 by How2Become Ltd.

Typeset by Gemma Butler for How2Become Ltd.

Disclaimer

Every effort has been made to ensure that the information contained within this guide is accurate at the time of publication. How2Become Ltd is not responsible for anyone failing any part of any selection process as a result of the information contained within this guide. How2Become Ltd and their authors cannot accept any responsibility for any errors or omissions within this guide, however caused. No responsibility for loss or damage occasioned by any person acting, or refraining from action, as a result of the material in this publication can be accepted by How2Become Ltd. The information within this guide does not represent the views of any third party service or organisation.

Contents

Introduction

Many young people aspire to become members of Australia's police forces. While aspirations are one thing, successfully completing the application process and the selection process are quite another.

Not everyone is suited to the role of a police officer. Often, a police officer will have to put the safety of others before the safety of themselves, and they must always bear the public's interest and wellbeing in mind. Police officers need to be physically and psychologically fit in order to perform their job properly. For this reason, the selection process is incredibly stringent, and will ask a lot of any candidate who wishes to apply.

Having said this, do not let the challenge put you off your dream career. Joining any police service will be tough, but the benefits of being a police officer are tremendous. The training is strenuous but rewarding, and a whole world of career opportunities can open up once you have completed the selection process. Additionally, police officers work alongside like-minded individuals in an environment which demands respect for one another. It's also a career that pays well and offers a lot of holiday and leave time, respecting the work-life balance of officers.

Whether you are interested in a career with the Australian Federal Police (AFP), or you aspire to become a sheriff's officer, bailiff, or a member of a certain state's police force, you must first meet several minimum requirements. These include having a valid driver's license and a first-aid certificate. The minimum requirements for becoming a police officer in Australia are detailed in chapter 2.

You must then complete an application that will be reviewed prior to the selection process. The application stage is only the first step of many, but taking the time to fill it out thoughtfully and thoroughly is absolutely vital if you hope to move forward with the selection process. Details on passing the application stage can be found in chapter 3.

During the selection process itself, you will take a number of tests, that are specifically designed to assess your mental, physical, and emotional capacities. If you pass those tests successfully, you will move forward to the interview process. Information on these tests can be found in chapters 4 and 5.

Candidates who make it to the interview stage will be asked a series of questions to get a better understanding of yourself in person. By this point, your potential employers probably have a general idea with regards to your physical and mental aptitude, as well as your beliefs and attitudes. The interview stage is a candidate's chance to back up their performance with great interpersonal skills.

Before continuing to look at the application process, it is important that you learn how the different police services in Australia operate. While you might not be tested on the history of these forces, it is helpful to know their stories, since this will round out your knowledge, and perhaps draw you to a specific service.

Chapter 1
The Role of Australia's Police Officers

Throughout Australia, law enforcement is facilitated by a number of different bodies, including police, bailiffs, and sheriffs. Additionally, there are a few agencies which specialise in white-collar crime, such as money laundering, embezzlement and racketeering. Each agency is responsible for enforcing the laws within the boundaries of its jurisdiction. For instance, the police are primarily responsible for the enforcement of criminal laws, whilst the sheriff's officers and bailiffs of each state enforce civil law.

Each state has its own police force, which is responsible for the enforcement of state laws and city statutes, while the Australian Federal Police are responsible for investigating any crimes against Commonwealth laws, as well as for community policing in conjunction with local agencies. All agencies co-operate with one another, occasionally transferring cases between one another, depending on existing circumstances.

Australian Federal Police (AFP)

The Australian Federal Police, or AFP, is an international law enforcement agency tasked with enforcing criminal law within the Commonwealth of Australia and protecting its interests overseas. Formed on 19th October 1979, it merged the former Commonwealth Police, the Australian Capital Territory Police, and the Federal Bureau of Narcotics. It is held within the portfolio of the Home Affairs Ministry, with its key priorities being set by the Australian Minister for Home Affairs.

The AFP provides community police services to the Australian Capital Territory, the Jervis Bay Territory, Christmas Island, Norfolk Island, the Cocos Islands, and it maintains an extensive international liaison network, with officers occupying 33 different international posts. Consisting of a workforce of more than 6,500 individuals, the AFP focuses on illicit drug trafficking, human trafficking, fraud against the government, organised crime, money laundering, and high-tech crime. In addition, the AFP prevents, counters, and investigates acts of terrorism. Keeping the peace and preserving public safety are top priorities.

The AFP is also home to the Specialist Response Group, an elite unit focused on providing tactical solutions to high and critical risk incidents. This includes disaster response, restoration of law and order, and bomb response.

The AFP also maintains a world-renowned Ceremonial Team, which includes the AFP Ceremonial Mounted Cadre and the AFP Pipes and Drums, who perform ceremonial duties at a number of functions and ceremonies.

State Police

Each state within the Commonwealth is responsible for maintaining its own police force, as is the Northern Territory. State police are responsible for maintaining law and order and handling traffic incidents and accidents, as well as for handling crimes. Water police, search and rescue personnel, and anti-terrorism experts are some of the specialists who are employed by various state police agencies. In some states, local governments employ additional officers called by-laws officers to handle matters such as parking, dog ownership, retailing, and other specific laws and ordinances. Many by-laws police are appointed as special constables or have been granted authority by local legislators.

State police perform many functions on behalf of the Australian government, including enforcement of Commonwealth Acts and Regulations. In sparsely populated areas, they also handle Sheriff's duties.

New South Wales Police Force

Formed in 1862 after the passing of the Police Regulation Act, the NSW Police Force is the longest-standing and currently the largest police force in Australia. It merged with the NSW Police Department following the Police Act of 1990, creating the NSW Police Force we see today.

With just under 17,000 staff and over 500 police stations, the NSW Police Force is more than a noteworthy part of Australia's police force. It serves seven million civilians over 801,000 square kilometres of land, making it one of the biggest police forces in the English-speaking world.

Northern Territory Police

Policing in the Northern Territory has existed since 1870, but the Northern Territory Police known today was founded in 1911. In the past fifty years, the number of police officers operating in the Northern Territory Police has grown from less than one hundred to over 1,300. It serves a population of 229,000 over a vast 1.3 million square kilometres and is host to a number of specialist groups.

Queensland Police

Queensland State broke away from New South Wales in 1859, and founded its first police force in 1864. It began with less than 150 employees, but by 2012 it would employ over 15,000 staff, 10,000 of which are police officers.

Based in Brisbane, the Queensland Police Force became the Queensland Police Service and serves five different regions in Queensland.

South Australia Police

The South Australia Police was formed in 1838, making it the oldest police force in Australia and among the oldest police services in the world. With 138 stations across over 1 million square kilometres, the 5,000 officers serve a population of approximately 1.7 million people.

Tasmania Police

With a jurisdiction of almost 70,000 square kilometres and serving 500,000 people, the Tasmania Police is relatively small compared to other police services and jurisdictions in Australia. Tasmania's police service employs approximately 1,600 people, including 1,200 officers.

Victoria Police

Established in 1853, Victoria Police currently serves almost 6 million Australians in Victoria State. It has over 14,000 sworn officers, as well as almost 3,000 civilian staff operating in 329 police stations. Community confidence in Victoria Police is very high, with over 75% of Victorians being satisfied with their police service.

Western Australia Police

West Australia Police was formally founded in 1853 when a Chief of Police was assigned to what was once a troop of mounted police. Today, it covers 2.5 million square kilometres of land, serving a population of 2.5 million with over 120 police stations. The Western Australia Police currently employs over 6,000 sworn officers as well as over 2,500 administrative staff.

Sheriffs and Bailiffs

Sheriffs and bailiffs are primarily responsible for recovering court ordered fines. However, sheriffs' and bailiffs' duties are not consistent throughout the states. Each state defines specific roles for employees of these departments. In the past, these departments were responsible for managing the gaols (jails), transporting prisoners, acting as coroners, and carrying out executions. Today, the departments deal primarily with the court system. Some common duties include:

• Maintaining court security;

- Seizing and selling the property of judgement debtors;

- Enforcing arrest warrants;

- Taking juveniles into custody;

- Handling evictions when necessary.

In some states, sheriffs are also responsible for enforcing drivers' licensing laws and auto registration laws, arranging for community service, and making arrests.

Council Rangers

Often referred to as 'local laws officers', council rangers enforce the by-laws of local government areas to, as well as enforcing certain state laws. Unless they are sworn as special constables, council rangers do not have full police powers. Often tasked with fire control, emergency management, enforcing off-road vehicle laws and dog ownership laws, their job description varies greatly from one local area to the next.

Other Police Agencies

A number of other police agencies are tasked with the enforcement of various laws and mandates; some of these agencies include regulatory agencies such as the Australian Fisheries Management Authority (AFMA). In recent years, many of these agencies have merged into larger departments, but a few specialised groups still exist. There are also multiple defence law enforcement agencies, including the Defence Security Authority (DSA), the Australian Defence Force Investigative Service (ADFIS), and the Royal Australian Corps of Military Police (RACMP).

What it Takes to Become a Police Officer in Australia

So far, we have discussed the different state police services, as well as the federal agencies recruiting in Australia. From the descriptions given, you might already have an idea of which police service (or services) you would like to work for.

While these agencies and forces may have slightly different focuses based on their expertise and location, all of them work towards the same goal of reducing crime and protecting civilians. Of course, this goal can manifest in multiple ways: a bailiff enforcing traffic laws and a counter-terror unit have vastly different training and experience, but are both working to enforce the law and protect people. Bear this in mind when making your application.

Chapter 2

Successful Applications: The Application Process

When applying for any new job, it is of utmost importance that you complete the application process correctly. When applying for a job as a police officer, the application holds an incredible amount of weight. Your ability to move through the rest of the selection process is determined by your ability to complete the application properly. Not only should you have a thorough understanding of the qualities that candidates must possess to successfully carry out the role of police officer, but you must also meet some specific minimum requirements.

Minimum Requirements

If you want to become a police officer in Australia, you must:

- Be over the age of 18;

- Have competed either Year 12 education or Year 10 with a trade certificate or similar qualification;

- Be an Australian citizen or New Zealand Citizen with a special category visa;

- Have a valid manual vehicle driver's licence;

- Be healthy and physically fit;

- Be self-motivated and willing to serve;

- Have a first-aid certificate;

- Have the confirmed ability to swim 100 metres freestyle, non-stop, clothed and unaided.

Some police departments have additional requirements. Before applying to any police department, it is advisable to learn which physical, educational, and other requirements applicants must possess. These details are readily accessible on each service's website.

Desirable Candidate Qualities

No matter which department you hope to apply for, you should be aware that all Australian police agencies look for the very best candidates possible. The testing and selection process are designed to weed out those candidates who do not meet minimum physical, mental, and emotional standards; candidates who excel in certain categories are understandably much more desirable than those who do not. Some desirable qualities for those who wish to take on the role of police officer include the following:

- **Honesty, personal accountability, and integrity.** Candidates will undergo thorough background investigations, to ensure that they meet the standards of the service.

- **A clean record.** While people with minor criminal convictions and traffic convictions are welcome to apply for positions, some convictions are serious enough to prevent an applicant from moving forward. If you have a conviction on your record, you should discuss it openly with recruitment personnel to find out whether it would affect your chances of successful selection.

- **Extra education or work experience.** Prior learning experience such as college credit will help your chances. In addition, if you have had some previous work experience, particularly work within some capacity of law enforcement, your chances of success improve. Whilst police departments offer academy training, some applicants are more desirable due to their maturity and past experiences. If you do not have any of this extra experience, it may be worth applying for some relevant courses or work experience before applying for a police officer role.

- **Undertaking and passing medical and drugs tests.** Prior to engagement, all successful applicants are required to undergo final medical examinations and testing for illicit drugs, along with a final security clearance. Maintaining a drug-free lifestyle and becoming as physically fit as possible is advisable.

Australia's police forces are committed to recruiting individuals from all of the diverse groups that make up Australian society. Your gender, ethnicity, race, sexual preference or other differences do not place you at any disadvantage.

How and Where to Apply

Applying for a police officer position isn't overly difficult, but there a number of things to consider before jumping in. First, you must decide which police department you wish to apply to. Some candidates place applications with multiple departments in order to speed up the process. This is a lot more work at the start of the process, but having a number of applications processing at once can be more time-efficient than applying for positions once at a time.

Before choosing a department or service to apply to, take some time to research what that department does. What areas do its officers work in? Where are officers stationed? What are their duty schedules like? What opportunities for advancement does the department offer? Many police departments offer career information sessions that can help make the decision-making process easier.

Putting serious thought into the application process not only helps you to make an educated decision about which department or departments to apply to, it also shows recruitment personnel within those departments that you are serious about your commitment. Taking the time to seriously consider which departments suit your personality and goals will show interviewers that you want the job. Ultimately, departments choose the candidates that are most likely to succeed; these are often the candidates who show the most personal initiative from the outset.

Once you have decided to begin the application process with a specific police department, you can begin your application. Many police departments offer online applications, and most departments have personnel specifically dedicated to recruiting new members. You may pick up an application at a jobs or career event, or you may simply print it out at home.

Be sure to know when and where to turn in your application. Applications completed online may be submitted online; some departments may ask you to submit your application in person. Other departments may request candidates submit their application by mail. In any case, double-check the requirements for sending in your application since it's the first step to your dream career.

Tips for Completing the Application Form

Unless you are completing your application online, make a few extra copies of your application. The reason for this is that you need to turn in an absolutely spotless copy to make a good first impression. Work on your application in a clean environment, away from anything that might spill on it, and ensure that there are no distractions as you begin the process of filling out required forms.

If you're completing online applications, keep multiple copies of any documents you need, preferably on multiple devices. Backing up your C.V. and any other application materials onto a USB drive means that if anything happens to your original copy, you still have another saved and ready to go.

Before beginning, take the time to read each of the questions carefully. Make a list of materials you might need to complete some areas of the application, such as:

• Your driving licence;

• Your birth certificate or other citizenship documents;

- Accurate information about previous employment dates and locations;

- Accurate information regarding education, including locales and dates;

- A list of trustworthy personal references including neighbours, friends, and relations.

The information that different departments ask for varies. Before beginning, be sure you have everything you need. Being prepared before starting is just the first step to filling out an application that will appeal to the police staff assigned to accepting or rejecting candidates.

Additionally, make sure that your application is well-presented and easy to follow. The staff assigned to reviewing applications will appreciate it if yours is organised, and might make you a preferable candidate in the process. After all, if they have trouble reading and understanding your application, a potential employer is less likely to see your qualities and therefore is less likely to offer you a job. For this reason, it is absolutely vital that you spend time making sure that all of your documents and materials are well-organised for your application.

In this chapter, you have learned the basics for filling in an application, such as the minimum requirements, desirable qualities and how to apply. In the next chapter, you will be familiarised with the top ten tips for sending off a successful application and making sure it stands out from the crowd.

Chapter 3
Ten Vital Tips for a Successful Application

Before filling out your application, ensure you have gathered all necessary materials as outlined in chapter two, and as required by the department for which you are applying. If you are applying for a position within more than one law enforcement agency, be sure that you have everything you need for completing all applications. Prepare in advance to take the stress out of the application process. Use the following tips and guidelines to craft an excellent application.

1. Schedule a Time and Place for Completing Applications

Just as you would with any other vital task, set aside a precise time and place for completing police applications. Be sure that you are well-rested before you begin, and ensure that you are comfortable; being hydrated and well-nourished can affect your performance. Being focused while writing your application will help you avoid silly mistakes such as misspellings and anything else which may cause confusion.

Police agencies use initial applications as a method for selecting the best candidates. Being at your best when you complete applications will ensure that you do the best you can, and it will make your application stand head and shoulders above applications from others who have never received or failed to follow this advice.

2. Read and Follow All Instructions Carefully

Before you touch pen to paper, be sure you have read all of the instructions given to you by the department. This is important for two reasons. Firstly, failing to follow a vital instruction could make your application void. For example, a department might require two photocopies of the same document in order to process your application properly. If a candidate failed to supply an extra photocopy, then the department would not be able to continue the application.

Secondly, failing to follow an instruction might not prevent the application from continuing, but may make it more difficult to process it. If this happens, all you are doing is showing that you have been unable to read the instructions carefully, which could impact your chances of success. Remember that you are applying to become a police officer, and with that comes the expectation that you are able to pay close attention to detail, as well as recognising and following instructions.

Once you have read the instructions, read all of the questions. Some questions may seem like duplicates, but you'll notice that they are in fact different from one another. Before writing or typing anything, consider your answers carefully. Remember, you are going to be judged on your answers, so they need to be as clear and concise as possible. Before writing anything into your application, jot down some notes on some scrap paper so that you can gather your thoughts. Remember not to hand these notes in with your application.

If you are going in-person to fill out an application, bring high quality blue and black ink pens with you. Some departments ask applicants to use blue ink, whilst others prefer applicants to use black ink. Simply using the wrong type of ink can cause recruitment personnel to reject an application. As previously mentioned, this is because departments want candidates which can take note of instructions and follow them to the letter. Bring extra pens in case you run out of ink, and be sure that the pens are of the same brand. Going the extra mile to ensure that your application has a streamlined look will help you get noticed.

3. Select References Carefully

Before going to fill out an application, or before working on an application at home, be sure that you have selected a number of people to serve as personal references for you.

Ask in advance before using someone as a reference, and tell them that you plan to provide police recruiters with their names, telephone numbers, addresses, and e-mail addresses. If a person seems uncomfortable with this, find someone else to use as a reference.

Be sure you tell everyone you know that you plan to apply for work within the police force. If your application is selected and you move forward with testing, you will at some point be put through a complete background investigation for security purposes. Police detectives assigned to conduct background checks on applicants are thorough, often seeking out childhood friends, old neighbours, and distant relations to quiz about the way the applicant conducted himself or herself throughout life. Making sure that your acquaintances, friends and relatives are aware of this might be helpful.

4. Never Bend the Truth

Do not, under any circumstances, lie on your application. Do not bend the truth, not even a little bit. Police officers are human beings. They have often made mistakes in their lives. Some of them may have made the same kind of mistakes that you have made before they were police officers.

Police recruiters and background investigators know that teenagers often drink while underage or experiment with drugs. Most people have received some kind of traffic ticket in the past, or have been reprimanded for minor misdemeanours. Errors are part of being human. So long as you learned from your mistakes, paid fines, or took other action as necessary to correct your behaviour, you should be fine.

So, if an application asks whether you have tried marijuana, and the answer is "yes", be sure to answer truthfully. Be honest about answering follow-up questions, such as "When was the last time you used marijuana?" "How often did you use marijuana?" Do not try to cover up the truth about your past. Police services cannot tolerate dishonesty since officers have such a huge responsibility in society. Therefore, you must not lie or bend the truth during any part of your application. If you did lie, and the truth came out, there could be severe consequences. Practising honesty from the start is essential.

5. Be Prepared to Explain Answers

Be prepared to answer questions about your background, and be ready to provide honest answers to explain past behaviour and to explain the ways in which you have changed, if applicable. In some cases, you might fill out an application one day and be contacted by a background investigator the next. Be completely honest and open in answering inquiries.

Be prepared to be consistent. Investigators look for inconsistencies as a method for weeding out undesirable candidates. Be sure names, dates, and other information is correct on your application, and keep information with you so that you can provide follow-up answers if necessary.

Police agencies are now checking social media sites to see what applicants have posted in the past, and some things that you deleted might still be accessible to background officers. Be ready to answer questions about your social media activity.

6. Avoid Common Mistakes

There are a number of common mistakes that people make when turning in police applications. Avoiding these mistakes can help make your application shine.

- Don't cross anything out, and do not scribble, either. This is why you should get at least two copies of the application; get at least one for practise, and complete a perfect copy to turn in. Writing your answers down on note paper before writing them properly on the application can help avoid this mistake.

- Do not leave any spaces blank. If something does not apply to you, write "Not Applicable" or "N/A".

- If writing an application by hand, complete it neatly. Many police agencies have applicants complete forms by hand so that they can see how your handwriting looks. Do not write in script; write in print instead. Strive for a neat and consistent style.

- Do not work too fast. Focus on what you are doing, and shut out any distractions. Even though this is a relatively simple task, it needs to be done perfectly.

- If there are essay questions, be sure to think carefully before providing an answer. Some essay questions have more than one answer block to complete; reading the application before beginning can help you to complete each block correctly.

- When completing applications online, be sure that you click all submission buttons carefully and ensure you save any confirmation information that pops up. In addition, consider saving your answers on a separate document so you can re-submit with ease, if necessary.

- If mailing your application, ensure that the envelope you use looks just as good as the application it contains.

7. Check Your Spelling and Punctuation

Proofreading work can often feel like a chore, and sometimes it can be painful to read over what you've written. However, it's likely that you've probably made a mistake somewhere in your application, and proofreading your work will allow you to pinpoint any errors in your work.

Some of us just need a little extra help in the spelling and punctuation department. If you know for a fact that your writing skills are not quite up to par, consider taking a remedial course before you even apply to work with a police department. A big part of the job of police officer is to write detailed reports about incidents, accidents, and crimes. Spelling and punctuation are vital skills for success in fieldwork, just as they are for desk jobs.

If possible, give your application to a trusted friend or family member, and ask that person to look for errors. Often, a fresh pair of eyes can spot errors that you've missed; having those eyes belong to a friend or relative is much better than allowing police personnel to find your mistakes. This way, you can spot and correct any errors or ambiguities in your application.

If you are filling out a physical application (i.e. on paper), then re-write the entire application if you find mistakes. The effort will pay off in the end. Remember to continue to focus on turning in a quality copy, even if you are writing information for a third or fourth time.

8. Ensure You Attach Any Required Documentation Correctly

Many police agencies require candidates to turn in additional documentation with their applications. Some ask that additional pages are stapled to the application, while others ask applicants to use paper clips or place all documentation in a certain type of folder. Do not neglect these requirements.

In addition, be sure that any copies you turn in are of good quality. If your copier at home is not the best, go to an office centre and pay a small fee to make good copies. Ensure that documents have straight, clean edges, and check that they are completely readable. Again, if you are unsure whether they are easy to read, have a family member or friend look at your application to see if anything needs to be printed again. A second set of eyes will spot any documents which are difficult to read.

Double check to ensure you include all necessary documentation. Take a few minutes to make sure that you have every document necessary for the application, including extra copies if required. The easier you make recruiters' jobs, the better your chances of success. Don't just tell them why you're a great candidate, do all you can to prove it.

9. Turn Your Application In On Time

Often, police departments accept applications during specific time periods. If you hope to gain employment during a specific time span, then be sure you know when the deadline for turning in applications is. If you're applying and it's close to the end of one hiring period, consider waiting until the beginning of the next hiring period to turn in your application. You want your application to be noticed, not tossed onto a growing heap of last-minute paperwork.

Do not wait until the last minute to turn in your application. If you do this, not only will your application find its way to the bottom of the heap, it will be read by someone who has read hundreds or thousands of applications before getting to yours. Turning your application in well in advance of a deadline shows that you possess initiative and self-confidence, both of which are desirable qualities to display.

10. Follow Up if Possible

Most police departments have dedicated recruitment staff who are happy to answer inquiries from applicants. If you know where your application went, and if you know who read it, it is a good idea to call or e-mail with a short follow up, thanking that person for taking the time to read your application.

The reason for this is that the selection process can be gruelling for police recruiters, and selecting the right number of applicants to move forward in the process can be tough. There are many qualified candidates to consider, so putting in a little extra effort can really pay off in some cases.

In some cases, follow-up is discouraged. If there are specific instructions that advise candidates not to call or email recruitment staff, then follow those instructions.

In almost all cases, everyone who applies receives a response, either informing them that they have been selected for testing, or that their application has been rejected.

Be sure to follow these ten tips when writing your application. Take your time, think carefully about the questions and answer them truthfully. If your application is successful, you will be informed by the department you applied to with what comes next in the selection process. This will be the focus of the next chapter.

If your application is unsuccessful, it may be worth contacting the department and asking for feedback. Ask what prevented your application from succeeding, and then try to focus on those weaknesses and make them your strengths for the next application. Don't give up – give it another go at a later date.

Chapter 4
Understanding the Selection Process

Congratulations on making it this far and having your application accepted. Unfortunately, you're not out of the woods yet – the selection process contains a number of stages.

Once a police department has accepted your application, you will go through a demanding selection process that includes written testing, physical testing, and assessment, all designed to determine whether you have the mental and emotional fortitude required to be an effective member of a law enforcement team.

It is vital that you learn as much as possible about the tests prior to taking them, and it is also very important that you build yourself up physically in order to get great scores on physical aptitude tests. Not only will you be competing against hundreds of other applicants, you will be intentionally placed under increased stress, so that recruiters can gauge the way you react when under pressure.

Watch your health carefully during this time. Ensure you exercise properly and eat right. Get plenty of rest, and abstain from substances that could detract from your performance; alcohol, while completely legal, is one substance you should consider staying away from while you are in the midst of the testing and selection process.

While most police agencies' tests vary somewhat from one to the next, many are quite similar. You will need to check the specifics with the department or departments you are applying to; however, the following information will help you understand more about some of the most common types of tests that police candidates undergo during various portions of selection proceedings.

Written Tests

As previously mentioned, much of police work entails writing about details. Some police functions also involve mathematical equations. In addition, most police departments utilise a number of standardised forms. Written tests are designed to help police recruiters identify candidates who are capable of completing forms, performing simple mathematic equations, and writing cohesive sentences.

Most written tests of this kind include sections that cover reading comprehension, basic spelling and punctuation, basic science knowledge, some basic mathematics, and some short essay questions. Many departments and programs designed to aid police applicants through the selection process offer a selection of sample verbal reasoning tests, mathematical tests, and other tests as applicable.

It is very important to note that mechanical devices, such as calculators, are not normally allowed during testing. Neither are notes, cell phones, or other aids that could potentially skew a candidate's results. Most departments provide test materials, pencils, and scrap paper; nothing other than what is provided is normally allowed.

If it has been some time since you last took a written test, practising beforehand can be very helpful. Practice resources are easily available online and will help you discover your weaknesses, allowing you to turn them into your strengths for the actual test.

Remember that different police departments have slightly different tests, which may focus on different things. Make sure that you use the practice materials which match the departments that you are applying to.

Physical Aptitude and Agility Tests

Physical aptitude and agility tests are designed to ensure that candidates are fit enough to begin rigorous physical training. While there are certain standards which must be met, it is a very good idea to ensure that you can run faster, lift more weight, or complete certain activities better than the minimum requirements. All candidates are normally given complete information about what specific tests will consist of, well in advance of those tests being administered. In general, though, here are some very common aspects of physical testing:

- **Running.** Both short sprints and longer runs are usually part of physical aptitude testing. Distance and time varies from one department to the next.

- **Physical Strength.** There are a number of methods used to determine whether candidates possess the minimum physical strength requirements to successfully enter a police academy. These include grip strength tests, sit-ups, and push-ups; some departments may also have applicants demonstrate whether they are capable of lifting certain amounts of weight, or whether they are capable of dragging a heavy dummy for a certain distance.

- **Agility Testing.** Many departments require candidates to complete agility courses that include activities like climbing, crawling, and running, as well as carrying weight over a distance.

- **Skin Fold Testing and Body Mass Indexing.** Most departments will not hire a candidate or allow him or her to move forward with further testing if they are overfat. Requirements vary from one department to the next.

- **Eye Tests.** Some departments do not require candidate sight testing; others administer simple eye tests to check for vision acuity and colour blindness.

Recruits must meet certain physical and medical standards because police academy and the jobs police officers do are, by nature, physically demanding. Police officers must have the stamina to safely deal with emergency situations, shift work, and everyday tasks.

Psychological Evaluation Tests

Psychological evaluation testing is sometimes administered concurrently with physical evaluation tests; however, this testing may also be administered at a separate site on a different date. Behavioural tests are designed to allow administrators to look for both positive and negative personal psychological aspects in order to select those candidates whom are best suited to employment within police departments. Various aspects of the tests focus on qualities such as:

- **Integrity.** Are you consistently honest with yourself and others? Would you be a positive role model for the community? Are you capable of setting aside self-interest when necessary?

- **Leadership.** Are you able to lead, guide, or influence other people by setting a positive example, using logic and facts, or delegating activities to others? Would you be an asset to a team? Can you accept personal accountability for your actions?

- **Decisiveness.** Are you capable of making speedy decisions based on the information available? Are you able to implement plans and focus under duress?

- **Stress Management.** Can you remain objective and solve problems under urgent time constraints or while managing rudeness, aggression, or danger?

- **Compliance.** Are you able to follow standard instructions, procedures, and routines in an environment that is governed by strictly outlined policies and procedures? Can you complete necessary documents in accordance with regulations?

- **Problem Solving.** Using job skills, judgement, and training, are you capable of gathering facts, determining options, and drawing sound, logical conclusions prior to implementing any action? How does personal emotion play a role in your problem-solving skills? Do you suffer from anxiety that hinders astute problem solving?

- **Flexibility.** Can you find more than one way to solve a problem?

- **Communication.** Are you an effective verbal communicator? How well do you pick up on social cues? How are your interpersonal skills?

- **Organisational Awareness.** Are you capable of managing a number of complex tasks? How are your personal planning skills?

Some aspects of psychological testing will be verbally administered, and others may be given as written tests. For example, the Occupational Personality Questionnaire assesses candidates with respect to their capacity for coping with the responsibilities police officers face on a daily basis.

Interviews

There are a number of different types of interviews you may be submitted to during the selection process. These interviews often progress in difficulty. As you make your way through the process you may find yourself sitting or standing before a number of different police officials.

In some respects, these interviews are very much like other pre-employment interview proceedings that you may have been through in the past. Interviews provide you with an opportunity to do more than just show officials why you are a quality candidate; they allow you to verbally explain why you are a good choice for the job.

Background Checks

In today's world, no employer can be too careful; potential police recruits and other security personnel have traditionally been asked to submit to extensive background checks, and that is still true today.

Expect to fill out a very long questionnaire about all aspects of your personal life, your educational background, any questionable incidents you may have been involved in, and details regarding personal relationships.

The next chapter will discuss assessment centres, which you may be asked to attend during the selection process.

Chapter 5
How to Pass the Assessment Centre Tests

Attending an assessment centre is often part of the selection process, particularly if you are planning to apply to the AFP. If you must attend an assessment centre, prepare yourself for a long day by getting plenty of sleep the night before, and by taking good care of your health beforehand as well.

Be sure to get everything ready the day before you must leave to attend the assessment centre. You will be given a complete list of items to bring with you, which might include different documents and different types of clothing. Preparing in advance and double-checking everything on your list will ensure that you do not forget anything, and it will reduce your initial stress level. Be sure that you do not bring anything listed as "prohibited" to the test site with you.

A number of assessment techniques will be presented in a structured combination that allows for fairly quick, yet completely comprehensive assessment of each candidate. During the assessment process, you will very likely be interviewed, and you'll participate in written exercises. You may also participate in group discussions, along with individual presentations and psychological testing.

Once the assessment centre process has been completed, you will be advised of whether you are progressing to the next stage or not. If you are unsuccessful at assessment centre testing, you may re-apply during the next intake period.

Whether you attend an assessment day or an assessment centre, or if your tests take place over a more extended period of time, it is very important to remember to relax, breathe easy, and just be the very best version of "you" that you can be. The tests are specifically designed to physically, mentally, and emotionally elevate your stress levels so that officials can select the candidates who are best suited for the job of police officer. Reminding yourself of this fact can be helpful, and so can the following tips for each type of test.

Passing Written Tests

There are several ways to increase your chances of passing written police aptitude tests. The first and most important step is to find out what type of questions will be included on the test you are going to take. Most police departments provide specific information regarding what is on each section of every test. While they do not give hints about the exact questions that will be asked, they do provide quality samples that you can use to mentally prepare yourself.

For example, Victoria's Written Police Entrance Examination (PEE) consists of five separate types of tests:

- Language Comprehension and Spelling;

- English Skills;

- Writing;

- Reasoning Ability;

- Mathematics.

The South Australia Police Entry Exam is slightly different, consisting of six tests:

- Verbal Reasoning Ability;

- Non-Verbal Reasoning Ability;

- Grammatical Knowledge;

- Reading Comprehension;

- Written Questions;

- Spelling.

If the police department that you are applying to has a website, you can probably find and download a few sample questions there.

Some dedicated applicants find that taking police exam preparation courses is extremely helpful, and the majority of these people tend to do very well on the written portions of the exams. Of course, it is important to prepare for other types of testing as well since, in the end, you will be evaluated on merit of all the tests you took.

Success with Physical Aptitude and Agility Tests

In order to do well on physical aptitude and agility tests, you must be in good physical condition. If you will be taking the test in the same area you live in, and you train in that area, be sure to work out outdoors at least part of the time to simulate live conditions. If you will be taking the test at a higher altitude, then you should be prepared to encounter more difficulty with breathing, so exercise at a higher altitude whenever possible.

Remember that both your aerobic capacity and your level of actual physical strength will be tested, and keep in mind, your body mass index (BMI) will be calculated with calipers. In general, there are three types of physical tests you must successfully complete.

Body Fat Skin Fold Test. In this test, skin callipers are used to measure four different anatomical locations where fat tends to accumulate. If you are a male, your body fat skin fold percentage should be 20% or less for a high score. A percentage of 20% to 23.9% is considered to be marginal, and men with body fat skin fold percentages greater than 23.9% do not pass.

Females should have a body mass index of 30% or less for a perfect score. Scores between 30% and 33.9% are considered to be marginal, and scores of greater than 33.9% do not pass.

Multi-Stage Aerobic Fitness Tests. A common physical fitness test is the progressive 20-metre shuttle run, in which all applicants are required to reach the standard of 50% as per Australia's fitness norms.

Sprints and Distance Runs. Sprint testing and distance running may or may not be included in the testing procedure for the department you test with. Focusing your workouts on both speed and endurance can help you succeed with these tests as well as with the 20-metre shuttle run test.

Grip Strength, Pull-Ups, and Push-Ups. Depending on which department you test with, you may be required to pass physical strength tests that focus on hand grip strength, abdominal strength, and upper body strength. Most police departments publish their test requirements; if you know that you will be required to take these tests, practise in advance so that you can easily exceed requirements rather than meet them with difficulty. Not practising can lead to abject failure, meaning that all the time you have spent preparing thus far has been completely wasted.

Agility Test. A sample agility test used by the South Australia Police is as follows:

Beginning inside a police vehicle, applicants must first climb over a 1-metre mesh fence, followed by a climb over a 1.5-metre colour bond fence. Following this, they must climb over a 3-metre cyclone fence, and then climb over a 1-metre wire fence. Next, each applicant must crawl through a small opening before leaping over a 1.5-metre ditch, then running through a simulated car park. After climbing over two 1-metre hurdles, each applicant must climb through a window. Next, a 25 kg simulated body must be dragged for a distance of 20 metres. The dummy is then dropped, and the applicant runs for 120 metres. Finally, a car wheel is removed from the boot of a police vehicle, carried to the front of the vehicle, and placed on the ground; the wheel is then lifted from the ground and carried back to the rear of the vehicle, where it is once again placed inside the vehicle's boot.

These tests are timed, and often, police recruitment personnel add to the stress by yelling at candidates as they make their attempts. While you may not be able to simulate each of these tests perfectly, practising running, climbing, crawling, and lifting heavy objects can make all the difference to your success.

By losing any excess weight and by placing yourself on a solid physical fitness regimen, you can pass these physical fitness tests with flying colours.

Doing Well on Psychological Tests

The best way to prepare for psychological testing is to prevent yourself from becoming too nervous about the whole procedure. Anyone who is of a sound mind and who has an honest disposition tends to find that psychological testing is easy and even a bit fun.

Be completely honest as you answer written and verbal questions, and do not be surprised if you see the same questions a few times. This test is designed to help weed out anyone who is blatantly dishonest, or who is of questionable character. It is designed to help police recruitment officials look for signs of evasiveness, too.

Some of the questions you might be asked could involve asking you about certain situations that took place in the past. Be sure to provide honest answers, and be prepared to provide concrete evidence about the truthfulness of statements you provided. Do not succumb to the temptation to boast, and do not embellish anything, since some of these questions are designed specifically to provoke people who are prone to boasting or embellishment to slip up. Police officers must be honest. If you have trouble with honesty, work to improve your character before submitting to testing.

No matter what, be sure you are well rested and alert for your psychological evaluation. Try not to worry about what will take place; instead, just focus on providing truthful answers. Trying too hard to appear perfect will negatively impact your results, and can cause you to fail the test. The best way to pass a psychological test is to relax and be yourself.

Breakdown of Testing by State

As you will see, the police testing processes for each state are often very similar. Although each state uses a different combination of assessments in their selection processes, many of the same tests appear consistently – there is a lot of overlap. See below for a breakdown of the specific combination of tests that each state uses to assess their police applicants. Note: the following does not deal with the entire selection processes for the country's agencies, it only focuses on the testing aspect of these processes. Explanations and instructions for each of these tests will be found before the practice questions for each section.

Australian Federal Police

Cognitive Ability Assessments:

- Literacy Tests;

- Verbal Reasoning Tests;

- Numerical Reasoning Tests;

- Abstract Reasoning Tests;

- Spelling Tests.

New South Wales Police Force

Acer (Australian Council for Educational Research) Exams:

- Literacy Tests;

- Summary Writing Tests;

- Extended Writing Tests;

- Spelling Tests;

- Verbal Reasoning Tests;

- Abstract Reasoning Tests.

Northern Territory Police

Written Assessments:

- Reading Tests;

- Numerical Ability Tests;

- Writing Ability Tests;

- Problem-Solving Tests;

- Spelling Tests.

Queensland Police

Initial Online Assessment

Entrance Exam:

- Literacy Test;

- Listening Test;

- Spelling Test;

- Cognitive Test.

South Australia Police

Entrance Exam:

- Reading Ability Tests;

- Comprehension Tests;

- Numerical Reasoning Tests;

- Writing Ability Tests;

- Abstract Reasoning Tests;

- Spelling Tests.

Tasmania Police

Written Exam:

- Reading Ability Test;
- Numerical Ability Test;
- Writing Ability Test;
- Problem Solving Test;
- Job Suitability Test.

Victoria Police

Acer (Australian Council for Educational Research) Exams:

- Literacy Test;
- Writing Tests;
- Verbal Reasoning Tests;
- Abstract Reasoning Test;
- Oral Assessments;
- Computer Skills Test;
- Spelling Tests.

Western Australia Police

Police Entrance Exam (PEE):

- Verbal Reasoning Test;
- Abstract Reasoning Test;
- Audio Assessments;
- Audio/Visual Test;
- Writing Skills Test.

Here is a comprehensive list of all the written tests you could face when applying to any police agency in Australia:

- Reading/Literacy Tests;

- Verbal Reasoning Tests;

- Non-Verbal Reasoning Tests;

- Numerical Reasoning Tests;

- Writing Tests.

- Cognitive Tests;

- Comprehension Tests;

- Job Suitability Tests;

- Audio Tests.

So, as this list covers every police test in Australia, it will double as a contents page for our sample questions and answers section that will follow this chapter!

Sample Tests

Reading/Literacy Tests

Of course, being able to read to a reasonable standard is a vital requirement when applying to become a member of the police. Your ability in this area could be tested in a huge number of ways, so below we have included several possible methods of examination. Get started with the spelling section below.

Spelling – Sample Questions

Below are a number of multiple choice spelling questions. Fill in the gaps with the correct answers.

1. The Ofsted report implied that discipline could do with some
   _____.

   * Improovments
   * Inprovements
   * Improovements
   * Improvements

2. The team made a _____ to improving standards in the English department.

   * Comitment
   * Commitment
   * Committment
   * Comittmant

3. Students acted as _____ of the school during the trip.

   * Representatives
   * Reppresentatives
   * Reppressentatives
   * Representitives

4. _____ for the role were to be made by the 25th September.

- Aplications

- Applications

- Appliccations

- Applacations

5. The school adapted its schedule so that parents' evenings could occur more frequently than _____ .

- Anualy

- Annualy

- Annually

- Annuaily

6. There were no new additions to this year's Mathematics _____ .

- Curriculum

- Curicullum

- Curricullum

- Corriculum

7. Students were required to work _____ during this exercise.

- Indapendentily

- Independently

- Indipendantly

- Indipendently

8. Members of staff had _____ six weeks remaining to improve the quality of their students' handwriting.

- Approximately
- Aproximatly
- Approcsimately
- Approximatly

9. The constant _____ of students during lesson time was having a negative impact on their performance.

- Disapearance
- Disappeerence
- Disappearance
- Dissappearrance

10. Teachers were informed that they were to be harsh in disciplining _____ students.

- Abscent
- Absent
- Abbsent
- Absint

11. The staff are being observed to make sure that _____ demonstrating their points clearly.

- There
- Their
- They're
- Theyre

12. Only a few members of the class showed a _____ advancement in their understanding.

- Significent
- Signifficant
- Significant
- Siggnifficint

13. The project showed _____ progress.

- Demonstrabble
- Demonstrable
- Demonstrably
- Demonstrible

14. The sports teams had incredible _____.

- Deddication
- Dedicacion
- Dedication
- Dedecasion

15. Ramps were installed to _____ for students using wheelchairs.

- Accomidate
- Accommadate
- Acomidate
- Accommodate

16. Students were placed in _____ order for the class photographs.

- Hite

- Height

- Hieght

- Hight

17. The new lesson plans were _____ poorly.

- Received

- Recieved

- Receeved

- Reseved

18. The drummer in the school's jazz band held a spectacular _____.

- Rithim

- Rhithum

- Rhthem

- Rhythm

19. The group decided to do their biology project on _____.

- Capillaries

- Cappillaries

- Capilaries

- Capilliaries

20. Most of the staff were _____ with the new equipment.

- Enamored

- Enamoured

- Inamered

- Enamered

21. There were far _____ many people talking for anyone to be paying attention.

- To

- Too

- Two

- Tooo

22. Students were _____ by the documentary.

- Board

- Bored

- Bord

- Boared

23. There was no way of telling _____ bag belonged to Alex.

- Witch

- Whitch

- Which

- Wich

24. For the sake of _____, late arriving students were given extra time.

- Fareness
- Fairness
- Feirness
- Fairrness

25. Some of the younger pupils needed help with their _____.

- Pronunciation
- Pronounciation
- Pronownciation
- Prenunceation

26. They were _____ up to the task.

- Definately
- Definitely
- Deffinittly
- Definitly

27. _____ job will be to assist students who are struggling with Maths.

- You're
- Youre
- Your
- Yore

28. The school desperately needed a teacher who specialised in
_____.

- Triggernometry
- Trigonometry
- Trigganometry
- Trigenomatry

29. For security reasons, parents were no longer _____ to
enter school premises unsupervised.

- Aloud
- Alowed
- Allowed
- Alloud

30. It was only partially her fault, since she had been _____
by older students.

- Antaginised
- Antegonized
- Antagonnised
- Antagonised

Spelling – Answers

1. The Ofsted report implied that discipline could do with some **improvements**.

2. The team made a **commitment** to improving standards in the English department.

3. Students acted as **representatives** of the school during the trip.

4. **Applications** for the role were to be made by the 25th September.

5. The school adapted its schedule so that parents' evenings could occur more frequently than **annually**.

6. There were no new additions to this year's Mathematics **curriculum**.

7. Students were required to work **independently** during this exercise.

8. Members of staff had **approximately** six weeks remaining, to improve the quality of their students' handwriting.

9. The constant **disappearance** of students during lesson time was having a negative impact on their performance.

10. Teachers were informed that they were to be harsh in disciplining **absent** students.

11. The staff are being observed, to make sure that **they're** demonstrating their points clearly.

12. Only a few members of the class showed a **significant** advancement in their understanding.

13. The project showed **demonstrable** progress.

14. The sports teams had incredible **dedication**.

15. Ramps were installed to **accommodate** for students using wheelchairs.

16. Students were placed in **height** order for the class photographs.

17. The new lesson plans were **received** poorly.

18. The drummer in the school's jazz band held a spectacular **rhythm**.

19. The group decided to do their biology project on **capillaries**.

20. Most of the staff were **enamoured** with the new equipment.

21. There were far **too** many people talking for anyone to be paying attention.

22. Students were **bored** by the documentary.

23. There was no way of telling **which** bag belonged to Alex.

24. For the sake of **fairness**, late arriving students were given extra time.

25. Some of the younger pupils needed help with their **pronunciation**.

26. They were **definitely** up to the task.

27. **Your** job will be to assist students who are struggling with maths.

28. The school desperately needed a teacher who specialised in **trigonometry**.

29. For security reasons, parents were no longer **allowed** to enter school premises unsupervised.

30. It was only partially her fault, since she had been **antagonised** by older students.

Disagreement between Subject and Verb – Explanation

This is a form of cross-sentence incoherence which is the result of incorrect tense or singularity/plurality. This short explanation will cover the ways in which this grammatical error can appear, and the sample questions will appear underneath.

The first error occurs when two or more nouns are matched with a singular verb (e.g. 'was,' 'is'):

> *Gemma and Nazeem was the only people left in the hall.*

This is an error because the two nouns form a group, and therefore need a plural:

> *Gemma and Nazeem **were** the only people left in the hall.*

If the subject is a plural (i.e. two or more nouns grouped together) then the verb needs to be plural as well.

The second error appears when a plural determiner (e.g. 'some,' 'all,' 'less') is paired with a singular verb (e.g. 'was,' 'is'):

> *Fewer people has arrived on time than usual.*

The determiner 'fewer' is a plural, and 'has' is a singular verb. The verb needs to be changed to a plural:

If the determiner is a plural, then the verb must also be a plural.

> *Fewer people **have** arrived on time than usual.*

The next grammatical error is the opposite: when the determiner of the sentence is singular and the plural is a verb. The same rule applies – both need to be of the same kind:

> *This lesson were successful in conveying its key points.*

This should read as:

> *This lesson **was** successful in conveying its key points.*

Generally speaking, it's important that plurals match plurals and singulars match singulars. Keep an eye out for which appears in a sentence and then make sure every determiner matches it correctly.

Sample question

Circle the option in which the verb and the subject best suit one another.

Henry and Katie…

A. *was ready to work from the second that they entered the room. The rest of the group was struggling to organise themselves. The teacher weren't impressed by the chaos.*

B. *were ready to work from the second that they entered the room. The rest of the group were struggling to organise themselves. The teacher wasn't impressed by the chaos.*

C. *were ready to work from the second that they entered the room. The rest of the group was struggling to organise themselves. The teacher weren't impressed by the chaos.*

D. *was ready to work from the second that they entered the room. The rest of the group was struggling to organise themselves. The teacher wasn't impressed by the chaos.*

Disagreement between Subject and Verb

Henry and Katie...

A. *was ready to work from the second that they entered the room. The rest of the group was struggling to organise themselves. The teacher weren't impressed by the chaos.*

B. **were ready to work from the second that they entered the room. The rest of the group were struggling to organise themselves. The teacher wasn't impressed by the chaos**.

C. *were ready to work from the second that they entered the room. The rest of the group was struggling to organise themselves. The teacher weren't impressed by the chaos.*

D. *was ready to work from the second that they entered the room. The rest of the group was struggling to organise themselves. The teacher wasn't impressed by the chaos.*

The correct answer to this question is B. Since Henry and Katie are a plural together, the correct verb is 'were'. The second error comes after the word 'group' – this should be 'were' since certain members of the group ('the rest') are being singled out. However, had this read as 'The group ___ struggling to organise themselves', then the correct verb would be 'was' since the group is being referred to as a single entity. Finally, the correct verb for the teacher in this case is 'wasn't'.

Verbal Reasoning Explanation

Verbal Reasoning tests are used to determine a number of different aspects about a candidate.

This includes:

- How well you take in written information;

- Your understanding of grammar, spelling and punctuation;

- Your ability to choose between correct and false information;

- How well you understand the meanings of words;

- Your knowledge of different literary terminology.

ODD ONE OUT

Identify which word is the odd one out.

Question

A — Desk

B — Shelf

C — Cupboard

D — Chair

E — Wood

How to work it out

- The odd word out is 'wood'.

- All the other words are objects commonly made from wood. So wood is the word linking these words together.

Answer

E = Wood

WORD JUMBLES

*The word outside the brackets will only go with three of the words inside the brackets, in order to make a longer word. Which **ONE** word will it **NOT** go with?*

	A	**B**	**C**	**D**
Un	(adaptable	able	appropriate	afraid)

How to work it out

- Unadaptable
- Unable
- Unafraid
- **Unappropriate** is not a word. The correct term would be 'inappropriate'.

Answer

E = appropriate

COMPLETE THE SENTENCE

Complete the following sentence by adding in the correct word in the missing space.

The mechanic worked on the car for three hours. At the end of the three hours he was_____.

A	**B**	**C**	**D**
Home	Rich	Exhausted	Thinking

How to work it out

- The only word that makes sense would be 'exhausted'.

Answer

C = Exhausted

WORD FAMILIES

In each question, there are four or five words, your job is to pick out the word that links all the other words together.

A	B	C	D
Trousers	Clothing	Shirt	Skirt

How to work it out:

- You need to work out which word can group all of the other words to form a word family.

For the above example, 'clothing' is the word that links trousers, skirt and shirt, so therefore the correct answer would be B.

Answer

B = clothing

ANTONYMS / SYNONYMS

Work out what word means the opposite or the same as the word stated.

BEAUTIFUL

How to work out the antonym:

- Antonym means opposite, so you need to find a word that means the opposite to beautiful. For example, ugly.

How to work out the synonym:

- To work out the synonym for the above example, you need to find a word that means 'the same as'. For example, stunning.

COMPOUND WORDS

Find the two words, one from each group, that together make a new, real word. The word from the group on the left always comes first.

(MAN BEND SAUCE)   (TOMATO PAN DEN)

How to work it out:

- In order to work out these types of questions, you need to find a word from the left group to start off the new word.

- Eliminate the answers you know to be incorrect.

- You should realise, that 'sauce' and 'pan' can be put together to make the new word 'saucepan'.

Answer

Saucepan

CORRECT LETTERS

The same letter must be able to fit into both sets of brackets [?] in order to complete the word in front of the bracket, and begin the word after the bracket.

Question

Happ [?] ellow

Wh   [?] awn

A	B	C	D
W	H	Y	N

- The only letter that could fit inside the bracket in order to make 4 words is = Y.

- Happ**y**, **y**ellow, wh**y**, **y**awn

Answer

C = Y

ALPHABET PATTERNS

In each of the following questions, find the letters that best complete the series. The alphabet has been provided to assist you.

A B C D E F G H I J K L M N O P Q R S T U V W X Y Z

PW   [ ]   XO   BK   FG   JC

A – TS

B – ST

C – RS

D – TU

How to work it out:

• Let's take the first letter of each group and work out how it is progressing. Let's start with the third group (XO) because you need to work out a common pattern.

• You should notice that the first letter is moving up the alphabet four places (4 spaces from 'x' = 'b'). Once the pattern reaches the end, it begins back at the start of the alphabet.

• So to work out the first letter of the second group, take the first group and its starting letter 'p', and add four spaces (P + 4 = T).

• Now work out how the second letter is progressing.

• You should notice that the sequence is moving down the alphabet 4 spaces. (O = K = G = C).

• So the second group needs to go down from W, 4 spaces = S.

• So therefore the correct answer is TS.

Answer

A = TS

HIDDEN WORDS

A word is hidden amongst the sentence. It has four letters and is hidden at the end of one word and the beginning of the next word. What is the hidden word?

I need ice cold drinks during the summer time.

How to work it out:

• You need to find the hidden four letter word that is part of the ending of one word, and the beginning of the next.

• For this example, you need to pay attention to 'need' and 'ice'.

'nee**D ICE**'

Answer

Dice

CONNECT THE WORDS

In each question, there are two pairs of words. Only one of the answers will go equally well with both of these pairs.

(Look out for meanings of the words and other possibilities of how another word could be used in that situation).

(FALL TUMBLE)   (JOURNEY   OUTING)

A	B	C	D
Travel	Trip	Trap	Drop

• 'Travel' would not be appropriate because it doesn't fit with the first set of words.

• 'Trap' doesn't work because it doesn't fit with the second set of words.

• 'Drop' doesn't work because it doesn't fit with the second set of words.

Answer

B = trip (meaning to fall or stumble) or (taking a trip somewhere).

TOP TIPS FOR VERBAL REASONING!

♦ When taking Verbal Reasoning tests, some people like to work on the questions they find most difficult first. Some people prefer to leave the harder questions to last. Pick a way that you feel comfortable with, and use it throughout your Verbal Reasoning test.

♦ Accuracy is key. You need to remain as accurate as possible to ensure successful marks. That's why it is important to fully comprehend the questions and understand what is being asked.

♦ Make sure that you take the practice questions under timed conditions. This will help to better your overall performance by allowing you to practice under similar conditions to that of the real test.

♦ Make sure you read the question very carefully. Some questions are designed to trick you, so you need to fully understand what the question is asking you to do, before you answer it. We recommend that you read the question at least twice before attempting to answer it.

♦ Practice as many different *types* of Verbal Reasoning question as you can. Within this guide we have provided you with several different question types, in order to increase your understanding and enhance your performance. Please note, the question types within this guide are not exhaustive, they are merely a way to indicate the most common types of question found in the BTP Verbal Reasoning test.

♦ Practice a variety of difficulty levels. If you are undergoing practice questions and are finding them relatively easy, why not practice more difficult questions? This will allow you to boost your confidence and enhance your skills. If you practice a variety of difficulty levels, you will be ready to tackle any type of Verbal Reasoning question that you encounter in the assessment.

Verbal Reasoning Test

Question 1

What word pair has the most similar relationship to…

Colour : Spectrum

A	B	C	D
Verse : Rhyme	Waves : Sound	Tone : Scale	Nature : Atmosphere

Question 2

Which **one** word has a meaning that extends to or includes the meaning of all the other words?

A	B	C	D	E
Gymnastics	Swimming	Running	Training	Football

Question 3

A word is hidden amongst the sentence. It has four letters and is hidden in one word and at the beginning of the next word. What is the hidden word?

For the last time, I will not tell you again.

Answer

Question 4

Which word does not have a similar meaning to – imaginary?

A	B	C	D
Mythical	Fictional	Illusive	Fickle

Question 5

In the line below, the word outside of the brackets will only go with three of the words inside the brackets to make longer words. Which ONE word will it NOT go with?

	A	B	C	D
Un	**(affected**	**alike**	**adjusted**	**capable)**

Answer [   ]

Question 6

Which of the following words is the odd one out?

A	B	C
Forever	New	Fresh

Question 7

Which word is the odd one out?

A	B	C	D	E
Ostrich	Parrots	Penguins	Dodo	Owls

Question 8

In the line below, the word outside of the brackets will only go with three of the words inside the brackets to make longer words. Which **one** word will it **not** go with?

	A	B	C	D
Un	**(assuming**	**admired**	**usual**	**draught)**

Answer [   ]

Question 9

Four of the five sentences have the same meaning. Which **one** sentence has a **different** meaning?

A – Mike spent £180 during his shopping trip.

B – During his shopping trip, Mike spent £180.

C – The shopping trip cost Mike £180.

D – Mike made £180 from his shopping trip.

E – A total of £180 was spent on Mike's shopping trip.

Answer [   ]

Question 10

In the line below, the word outside of the brackets will only go with three of the words inside the brackets to make longer words. Which **one** word will it **not** go with?

	A	B	C	D
An	(tarctic	aerobic	ability	droid)

Answer [   ]

Question 11

Fill in the missing word so that the sentence reads correctly.

He _____ the telephone and then _____ it to his mother.

A	B	C	D
Heard / shouted	Answered / spoke	Picked / threw	Answered / passed

Question 12

Fill in the missing word so that the sentence reads correctly.

_____ *going to be in big trouble when they get home.*

A	B	C	D
Thair	There	Their	They're

Question 13

In the line below, the word outside of the brackets will only go with three of the words inside the brackets to make longer words. Which **one** word will it **not** go with?

	A	B	C	D
Imp	**(act**	**air**	**putter**	**ort)**

Answer [   ]

Question 14

Which of the following is the odd one out?

A	B	C	D
Trumpet	Violin	Harp	Guitar

Question 15

The following sentence has one word missing. Which **one** word makes the best sense when placed in the sentence?

A submarine is a vehicle that is _____ of independent operation underwater.

A	B	C	D	E
Evolved	Built	Capable	Designed	Submersible

Question 16

Four of the five sentences have the same meaning. Which **one** sentence has a **different** meaning?

A – It was a little girl who was pushed over by the tall boy.

B – The tall boy pushed over a little girl.

C – The little girl pushed over the boy.

D – The little girl fell over as a result of being pushed by the tall boy.

E – The tall boy got into trouble for pushing over a little girl.

Answer

Question 17

In the line below, the word outside of the brackets will only go with three of the words inside the brackets to make longer words. Which **one** word will it **not** go with?

	A	B	C	D
Im	(age	agine	moral	significant)

Answer

Question 18

The following sentence has one word missing. Which **one** word makes the best sense when placed in the sentence?

The man _____ he wanted to go home.

A	B	C	D	E
Chose	Needed	Decided	Ran	Boasted

Question 19

The following sentence has one word missing. Which **one** word makes the best sense when placed in the sentence?

The weather forecaster informed the public of the _____ rain.

A	B	C	D	E
Likelihood	Chance	Dry	Need	Potential

Question 20

Which of the following words is the odd one out?

A	B	C	D
Circle	Rectangle	Sphere	Triangle

Question 21

Which letter could be used to complete the four fragments of words below?

HER (_) RAG *and* BLUR (_) ALL

A	B	C	D
B	S	T	U

Question 22

Which of the following is the odd one out?

A	B	C	D	E
Rose	Lily	Daisy	Petal	Sunflower

Question 23

Which letter could be used to complete the four fragments of words below?

FEE (_) ARE *and* PLEA (_) ATE

A	B	C	D
D	L	S	Y

Question 24

Which of the following is the odd one out?

A	B	C	D
Now	Cow	Low	How

Question 25

In the line below, the word outside of the brackets will only go with three of the words inside the brackets to make longer words. Which ONE word will it NOT go with?

	A	B	C	D
In	**(decisive**	**reference**	**destructible**	**convenience)**

Answer [   ]

Question 26

Which four letter word can be placed at the **end** of the following words, in order to create four new words?

King   Parent   Adult   Priest

Answer [   ]

Question 27

Which four letter word can be placed at the **end** of the following words, in order to create four new words?

Accept   Like   Foresee   Adapt

Answer
[   ]

Question 28

If the following words were placed in alphabetical order, which one would be third?

A	B	C	D
Delightful	Delicious	Delayed	Delicate

Question 29

The following sentence has one word missing. Which **one** word makes the best sense when placed in the sentence?

He needed to be _____ for what he had done.

A – Helped

B – Reprimanded

C – Stopped

D – Maintained

E – Custody

Answer
[   ]

Question 30

Which of the following words is the odd one out?

A	B	C	D	E
Cup	Fork	Knife	Teaspoon	Spoon

Question 31

Which letter is missing from the following words?

taugh[?]   [?]hing   tigh[?]   [?]ile

A – T

B – S

C – E

D – N

Answer

Question 32

Which letter is missing from the following words?

skate[?]   [?]ace   clove[?]   [?]after

A – E

B – S

C – P

D – R

Answer

ANSWERS TO VERBAL REASONING TEST

Q1. C = Tone : Scale

EXPLANATION = for this type of question, you need to work out what two words have the most similar meaning to the two words shown. 'Colour' and 'spectrum' both can be related to 'tone' and 'scale'. Colours have different tones and can be defined on a scale i.e. light and dark; just like a spectrum has a scale and tones of colour.

Q2. D = training

EXPLANATION = 'training' is the one word that groups all of the other words together. Gymnastics, swimming, running and football are all types of training exercises for athletic sport.

Q3. Fort

EXPLANATION = '**for t**he'.

Q4. D = fickle

EXPLANATION = fictional, illusive and mythical are all words that relate to 'imaginary'. 'Fickle' does not carry the same connotations as these words and therefore does not have a similar meaning.

Q5. D = capable

EXPLANATION = if you were to put 'un' with the words 'affected', 'alike' and 'adjusted', you would get: unaffected, unalike and unadjusted. However, if you tried to put 'un' with 'capable', it would not be grammatically correct. Therefore, answer D does not go with the word outside the bracket.

Q6. A = forever

EXPLANATION = 'forever' is the odd one out because both 'new' and 'fresh' have a similar meaning.

Q7. D = dodo

EXPLANATION = all of the other words refer to birds that are not extinct.

Q8. D = draught

EXPLANATION = if you were to put 'un' with the words 'assuming, 'admired', and 'usual', you would get: unassuming, unadmired and unusual. However, if you were to put 'un' with 'draught', this would not be grammatically correct.

Q9. D = Mike made £180 from his shopping trip.

EXPLANATION = the other four sentences refer to Mike spending money, therefore answer option D (Mike made £180 from his shopping trip) means something different.

Q10. C = ability

EXPLANATION = if were to put 'an' with 'tarctic', 'aerobic' and 'droid', you would get: 'Antarctic', 'anaerobic' and 'android'. However, if you were to put 'an' with 'ability', this would not be grammatically correct.

Q11. D = answered / passed

EXPLANATION = He **answered** the telephone and then **passed** it to his mother.

Q12. D = they're

EXPLANATION = in order to find the missing word, you need to work out the sentence structure. Is it in past tense, present tense or future tense? The word that is grammatically correct for this sentence is 'they're'. So, the sentence would read 'they're (they are) going to be in big trouble when they get home'.

Q13. C = putter

EXPLANATION = impact, impair, import. Therefore the word that does not fit with (imp) is 'putter'. Impputter is not a word, and therefore does not fit with the word outside the brackets.

Q14. A = trumpet

EXPLANATION = trumpet is the only instrument listed that requires you to play using your mouth. The other instruments require you to play the instrument using your hands.

Q15. C = capable

EXPLANATION = the word that would best fit the sentence is 'capable'. So, the sentence would read 'a submarine is a watercraft capable of independent operation underwater'.

Q16. C = the little girl pushed over the boy.

EXPLANATION = the sentence 'the little girl pushed over the boy' has the opposite meaning to all of the other sentences, therefore this sentence is the odd one out.

Q17. D = significant

EXPLANATION = if you were to put 'im' with 'age', 'agine' and 'moral', you would get: 'image', 'imagine' and 'immoral'. However, if you were to put 'im' with 'significant', this would be grammatically incorrect.

Q18. C = decided

EXPLANATION = the correct word is 'decided'. So, the sentence would read 'the man decided he wanted to go home'.

Q19. E = potential

EXPLANATION = the word that is needed in order to make the sentence grammatically correct is 'potential'. So, the sentence would read 'the weather forecaster informed the public of the potential rain'.

Q20. C = sphere

EXPLANATION = 'sphere' is the odd one out because all of the other words refer to 2D shapes. A sphere is 3-dimensional.

Q21. A = b

EXPLANATION = *herb, brag, blurb* and *ball.*

Q22. D = petal

EXPLANATION = 'petal' is the odd one out because all of the other words refer to 'types' of flowers, whereas a 'petal' is part of a flower.

Q23. A = d

EXPLANATION = *feed, dare, plead* and *date.*

Q24. C = low

EXPLANATION = low is the odd one out, because it is pronounced differently from the other three words.

Q25. B = reference

EXPLANATION = if you were to put the word 'in' with the words 'decisive', 'destructible' and 'convenience', you would get: 'indecisive', 'indestructible' and 'inconvenience'. However, if you were to put the word 'in' with the word 'reference', this would be grammatically incorrect.

Q26. Hood

EXPLANATION = king*hood,* parent*hood,* adult*hood* and priest*hood.*

Q27. Able

EXPLANATION = accept*able,* like*able,* foresee*able* and adapt*able.*

Q28. B = delicious

EXPLANATION = in alphabetical order, the words would read as follows: *delayed, delicate, delicious* and *delightful.* So, the third word in the sequence would be 'delicious'.

Q29. B = reprimanded

EXPLANATION = the sentence would best read as follows: *'He needed to be* reprimanded *for what he had done'.*

Q30. A = cup

EXPLANATION = 'cup' is the odd one out because all of the other words are types of cutlery, whereas a 'cup' is an item of crockery.

Q31. A = t

EXPLANATION = *taught, thing, tight* and *tile.*

Q32. D = r

EXPLANATION = *skater, race, clover* and *rafter.*

Non-Verbal Reasoning Explanation

Non-Verbal Reasoning tests are often used to assess a person's ability to recognise shapes and patterns and their changing formations. The questions appear in diagrammatic and pictorial form, and can be broken up into 3 categories: **Abstract, Spatial or Inductive Reasoning.**

The importance of Non-Verbal Reasoning tests is to determine how well you can understand and visualise information to solve problems. You need to be able to recognise and identify patterns amongst abstract shapes and images.

Non-Verbal Reasoning tests have become a popular tool for job selection processes, so it is imperative that you get to grips with each question type and know how to answer them.

For psychometric testing, you need to aim for speed as well as accuracy. It is important to be able to undergo these tests with the utmost confidence and composure, in order to work swiftly and effectively throughout the test.

What Do The Questions Look Like?

The type of questions that you will face in the Non-Verbal Reasoning test will vary depending on the type of test you will be sitting. This chapter provides you with a variety of sample questions and explanations in order to give you a clearer understanding of what to expect.

Such tests may include:

• Determining identical shapes;

• Rotating shapes;

• Reflections of shapes;

• Finding the odd shape;

• Finding the missing shape;

• 3D shapes;

• Coding;

• Shading and colours;

• Number sequences.

Please note that Spatial Reasoning and Abstract Reasoning have similarities, but are also very different. Thus, it is important to know which type of Non-Verbal Reasoning test you will be sitting. However, practising all types of questions can only work in your favour and better your chances at gaining a higher score.

Abstract (or Diagrammatic) – are tests to measure general intelligence. These tests require you to evaluate the rules surrounding the diagrams.

Spatial Reasoning – are tests which work with detailed and complex plans. Often, they rely on mental rotations of shapes.

TOP TIPS FOR NON-VERBAL REASONING!

♦ Try to visualise the questions.

♦ **The Cube Questions** – why not make yourself a cube net as you try to work out the questions? This will help you to visualise where the shapes on the cube will be once you have folded the cube together.

♦ Non-Verbal Reasoning tests are designed to test people under strict time limits. Most people find it difficult to finish all the questions. Therefore, these tests are designed to measure people's level of accuracy whilst working in speedy conditions.

♦ Drawing or writing out your answers is a useful way to see what is going on. Drawing out the answers of what you think it may look like more clearly, will help you to visualise the answers.

♦ Using highlighters is a useful way of distinguishing your answers. Highlighting is helpful if you are counting lots of shapes or working out numbers of angles etc.

♦ **The Complete Grid Questions** – to make sure you have got the correct answer, you can always work backwards. By working backwards, you would have to do the opposite to what is being asked, but it is a useful way to check if you have the correct answer.

♦ Pay attention to everything! If you are unsure about what the differences are or what is happening in the sequence, pay attention to everything you see. Count all the sides, angles, colours, shading, line types, sizing, rotations, reflections etc. That way you can eliminate what is the same, and what is different about the sequence.

Non-Verbal Reasoning – Spatial Reasoning Test

During the following spatial reasoning exercise your task is to look at the given shapes and decide which of the examples match the shape when joined together by the corresponding letters.

Question 1

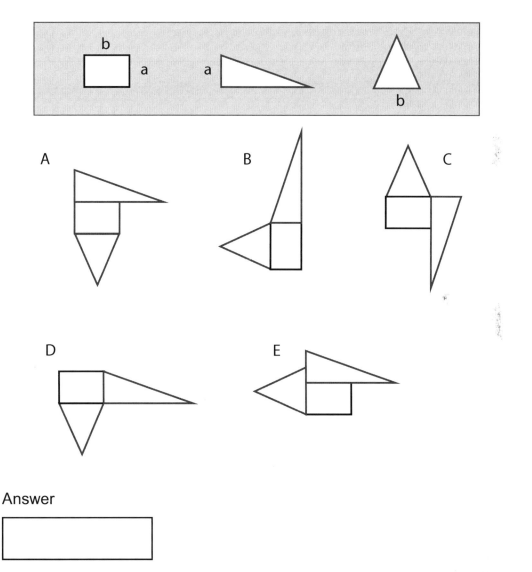

Answer

Question 2

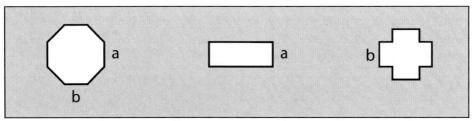

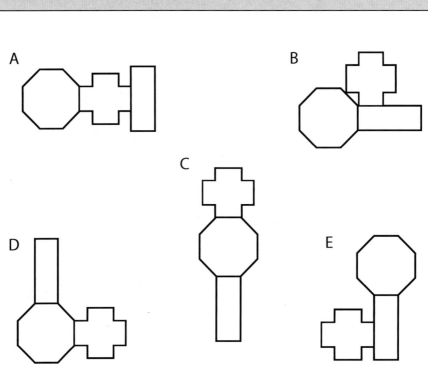

Answer

Question 3

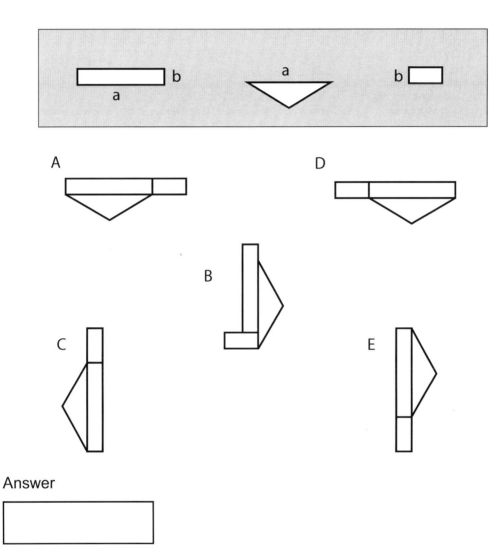

Answer

Question 4

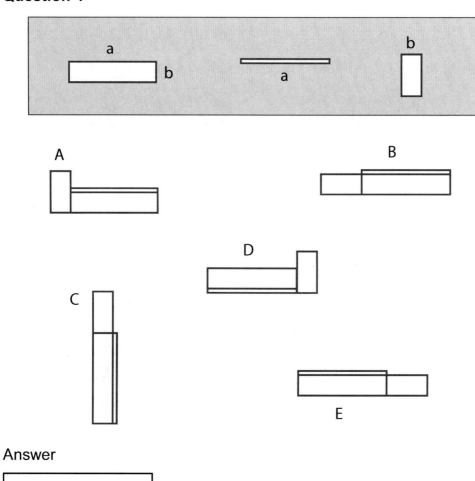

Answer

Question 5

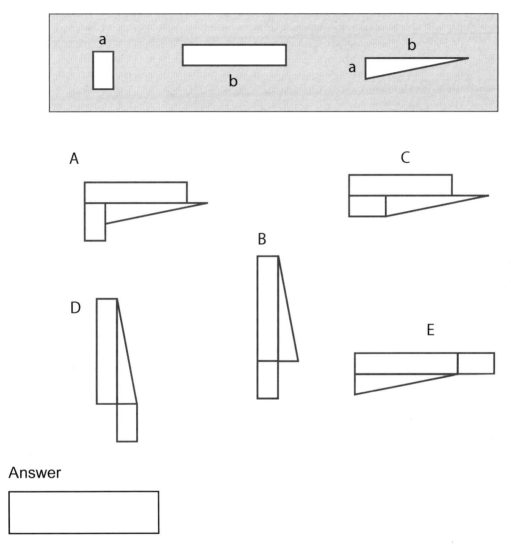

Answer

Question 6

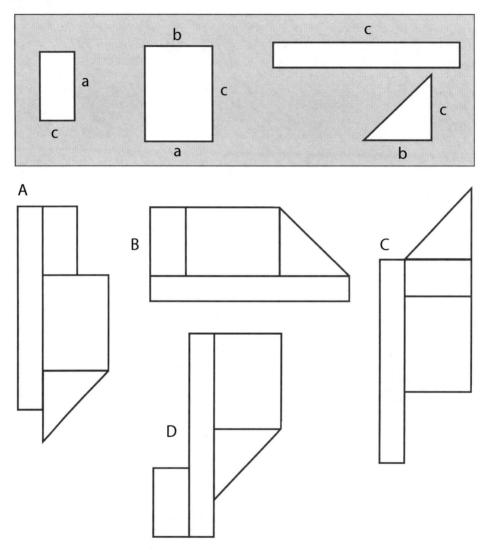

Answer

Question 7

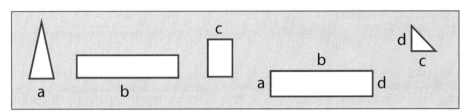

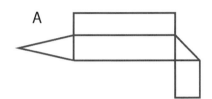

A

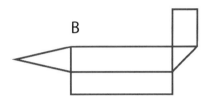

B

C

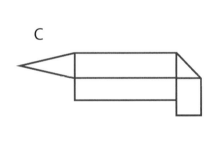

D

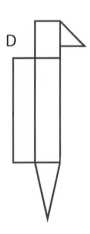

Answer

Question 8

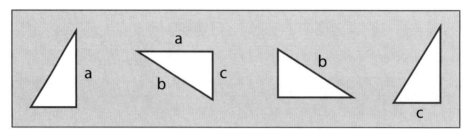

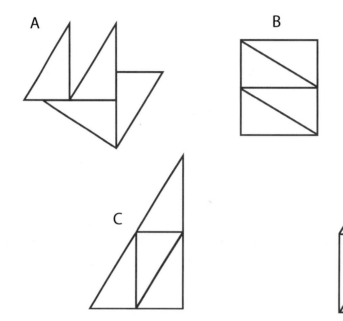

A

B

C

D

Answer

Question 9

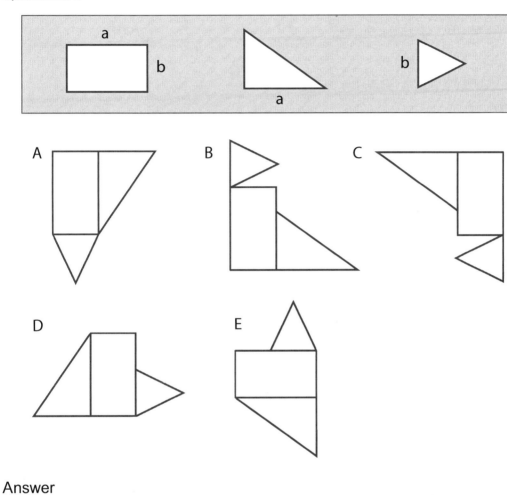

Answer

Question 10

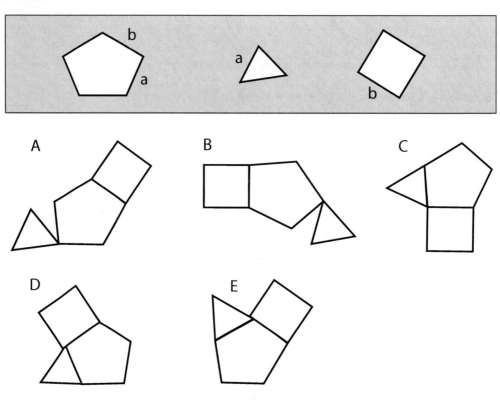

Answer

Question 11

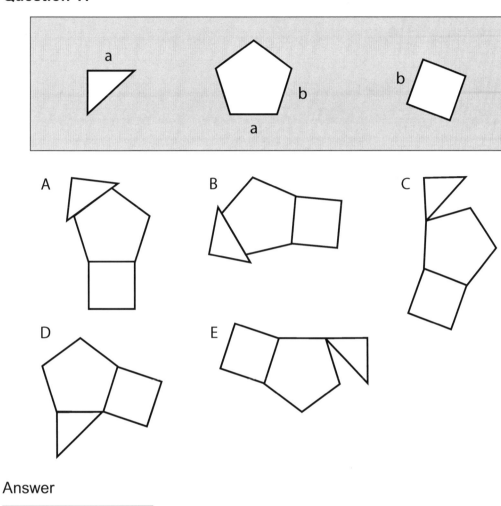

Answer

Question 12

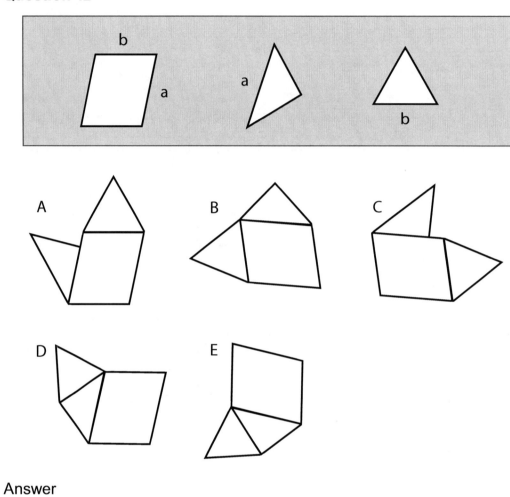

Answer

Question 13

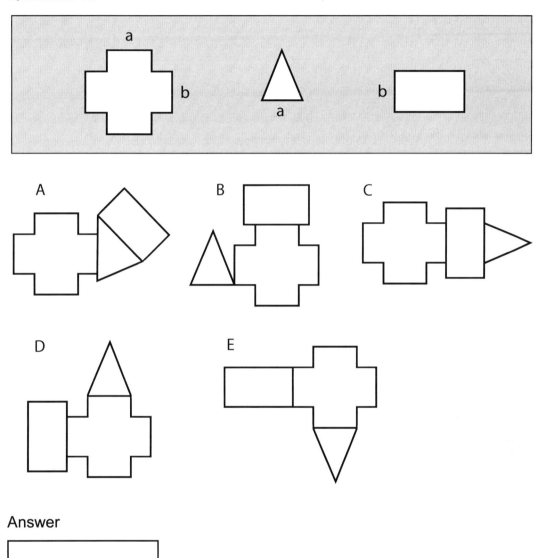

Answer

Question 14

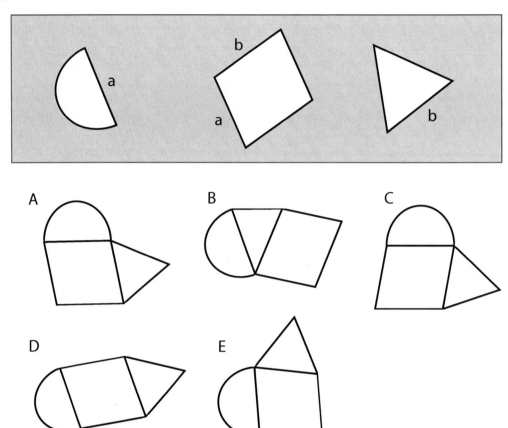

Answer

Question 15

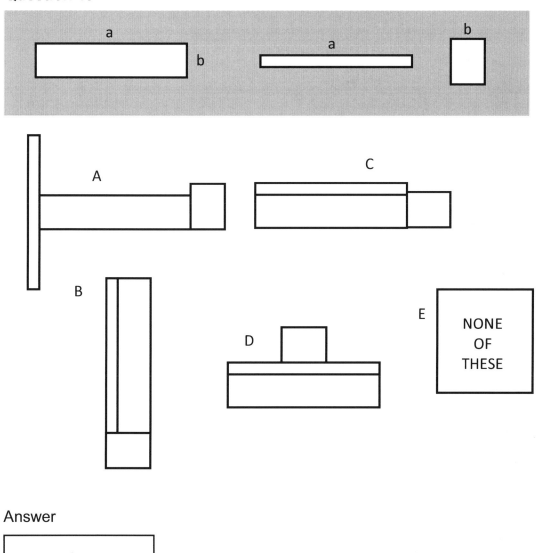

Answer

Question 16

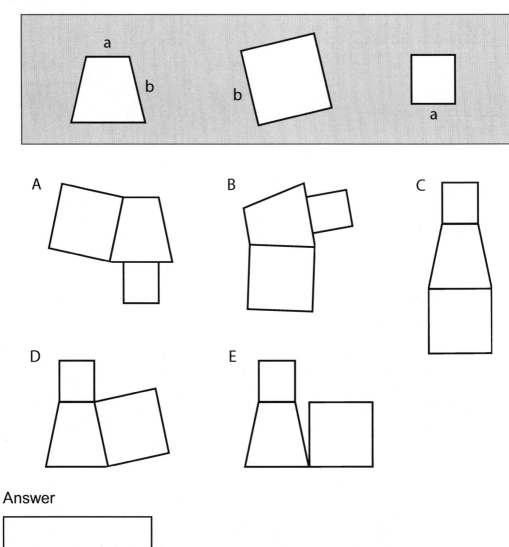

Answer

Question 17

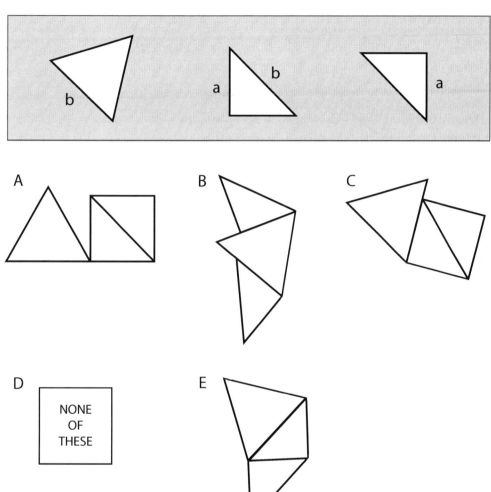

Answer

Question 18

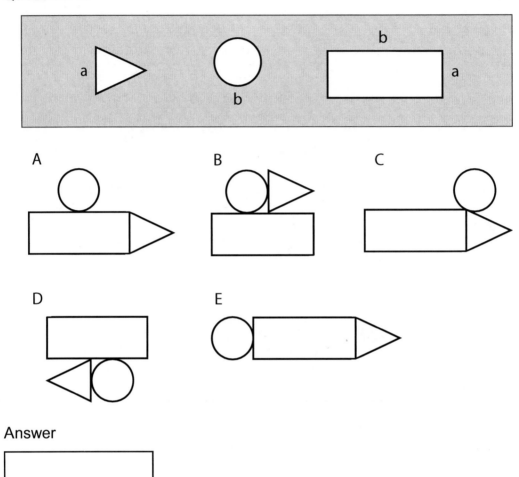

Answer

Question 19

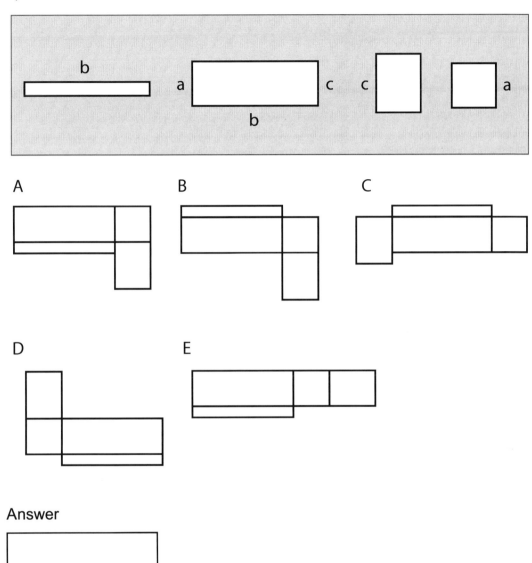

Answer

Question 20

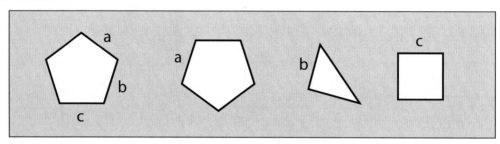

A

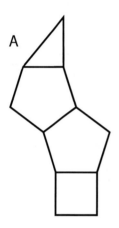

B

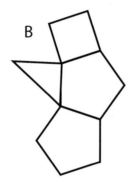

C

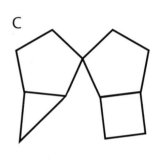

D

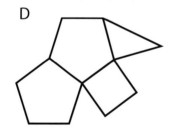

E

NONE
OF
THESE

Answer

ANSWERS TO NON-VERBAL REASONING – SPATIAL REASONING

Q1. B

Q2. D

Q3. A

Q4. E

Q5. D

Q6. B

Q7. A

Q8. C

Q9. A

Q10. C

Q11. D

Q12. B

Q13. E

Q14. A

Q15. C

Q16. D

Q17. E

Q18. A

Q19. C

Q20. B

Non-Verbal Reasoning – Abstract Reasoning Test

Q1. Which SET does the TEST SHAPE belong to?

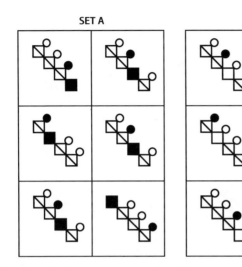

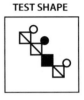

A	B	C
Set A	Set B	Neither

Q2. Which SET does the TEST SHAPE belong to?

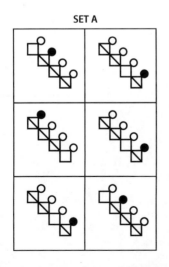
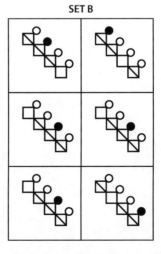

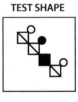

A	B	C
Set A	Set B	Neither

Q3. Which SET does the TEST SHAPE belong to?

SET A   SET B   TEST SHAPE

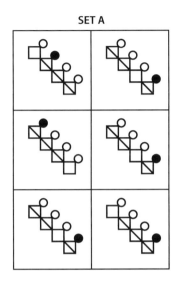 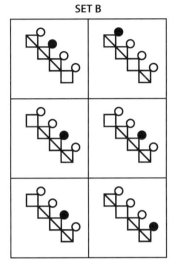 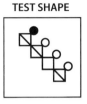

A	B	C
Set A	Set B	Neither

Q4. Which SET does the TEST SHAPE belong to?

SET A   SET B   TEST SHAPE

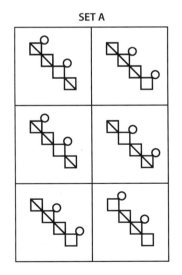 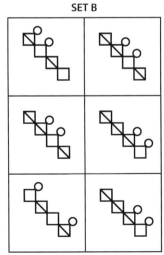 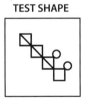

A	B	C
Set A	Set B	Neither

Q5. Which SET does the TEST SHAPE belong to?

SET A	SET B	TEST SHAPE

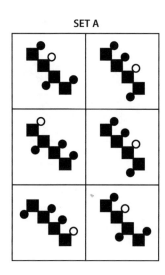 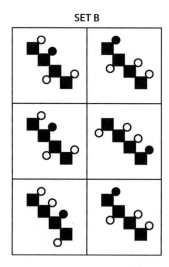 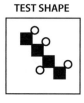

A	B	C
Set A	Set B	Neither

Q6. Which SET does the TEST SHAPE belong to?

SET A	SET B	TEST SHAPE

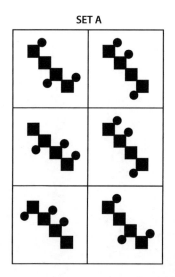 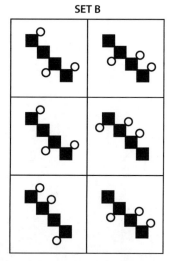

A	B	C
Set A	Set B	Neither

Q7. Which SET does the TEST SHAPE belong to?

SET A   SET B   TEST SHAPE

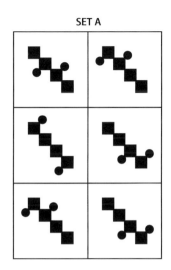 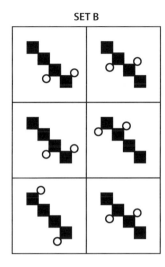 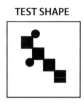

A	B	C
Set A	Set B	Neither

Q8. Which SET does the TEST SHAPE belong to?

SET A   SET B   TEST SHAPE

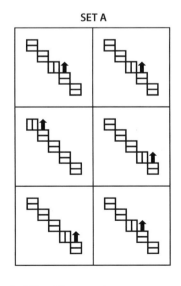 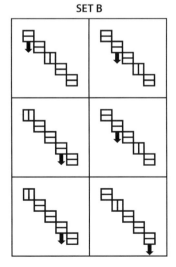 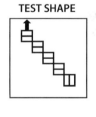

A	B	C
Set A	Set B	Neither

Q9. Which SET does the TEST SHAPE belong to?

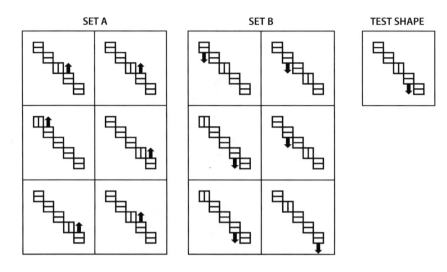

A	B	C
Set A	Set B	Neither

Q10. Which SET does the TEST SHAPE belong to?

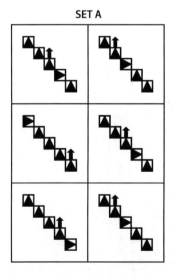 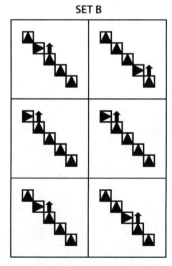 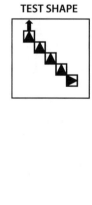

A	B	C
Set A	Set B	Neither

Q11. Which figure comes next in the series?

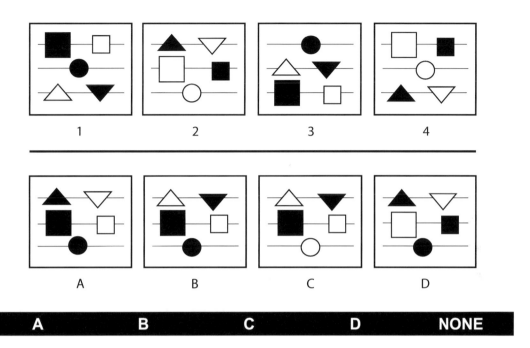

Q12. Which figure comes next in the series?

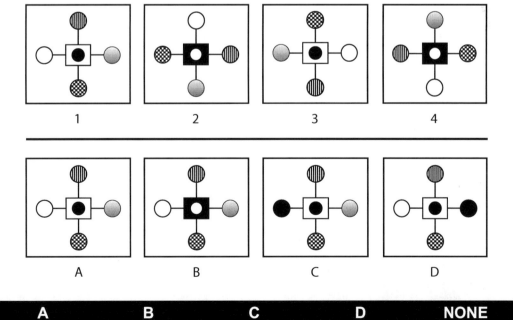

Q13. Which figure comes next in the series?

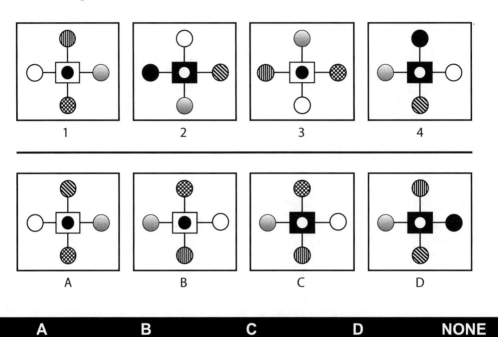

| A | B | C | D | NONE |

Q14. Which figure comes next in the series?

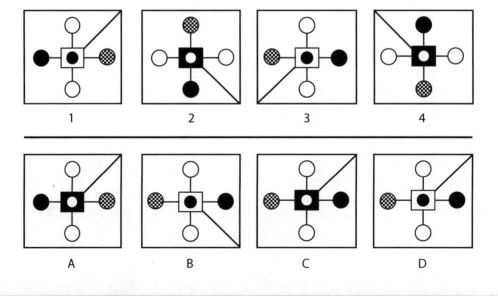

| A | B | C | D | NONE |

Q15. Which figure comes next in the series?

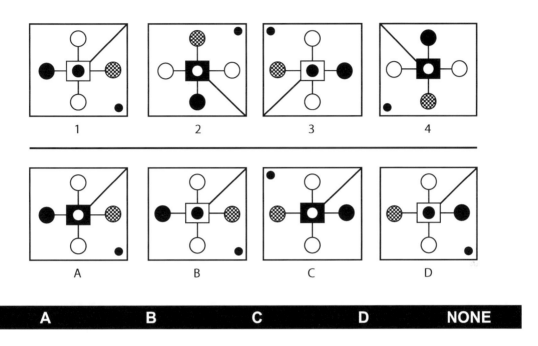

| A | B | C | D | NONE |

Q16. Which figure comes next in the series?

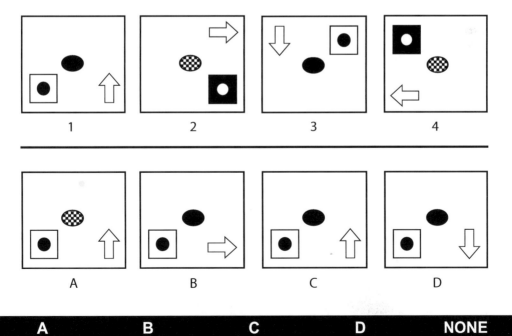

| A | B | C | D | NONE |

Q17.

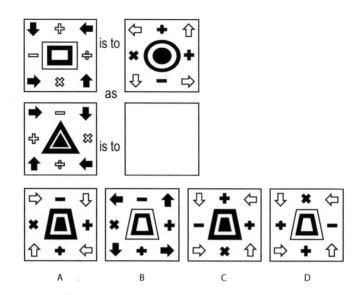

A	B	C	D	NONE

Q18.

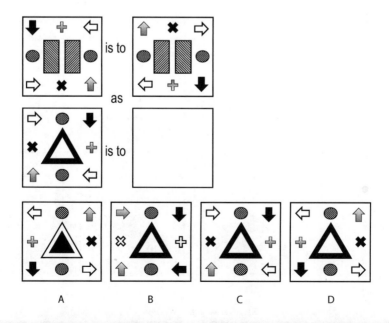

A	B	C	D	NONE

Q19.

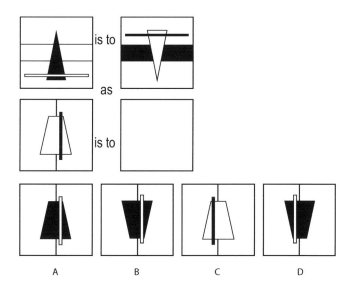

| A | B | C | D | NONE |

Q20.

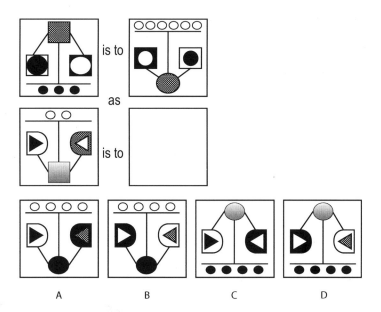

| A | B | C | D | NONE |

Q21.

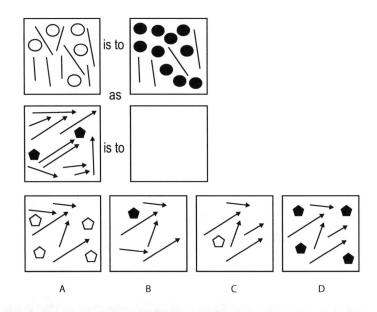

A	B	C	D	NONE

Q22.

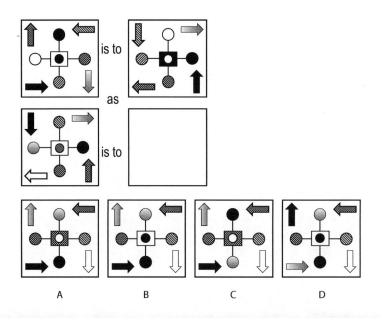

A	B	C	D	NONE

Q23. The middle row of boxes create a rule that has been applied to the boxes directly above them. Which answer option (A to E) corresponds to the rule under the box with the question mark?

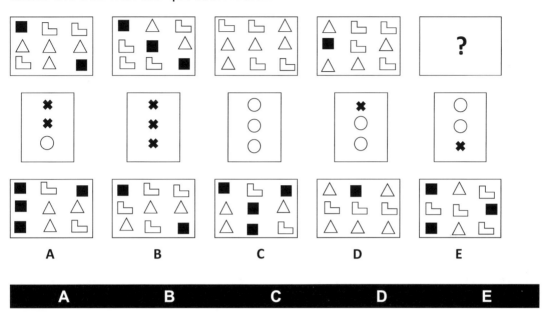

Q24. The middle row of boxes create a rule that has been applied to the boxes directly above them. Which answer option (A to E) corresponds to the rule under the box with the question mark?

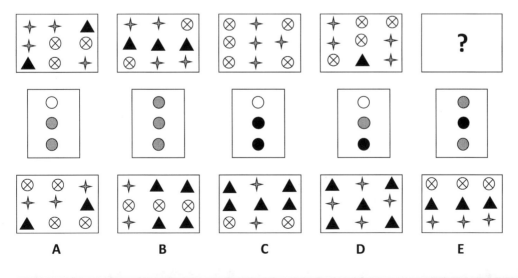

Q25. The middle row of boxes create a rule that has been applied to the boxes directly above them. Which answer option (A to E) corresponds to the rule under the box with the question mark?

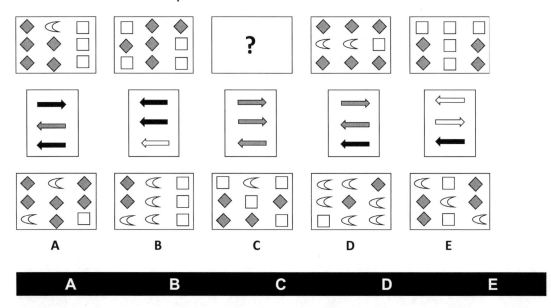

Q26. The middle row of boxes create a rule that has been applied to the boxes directly above them. Which answer option (A to E) corresponds to the rule under the box with the question mark?

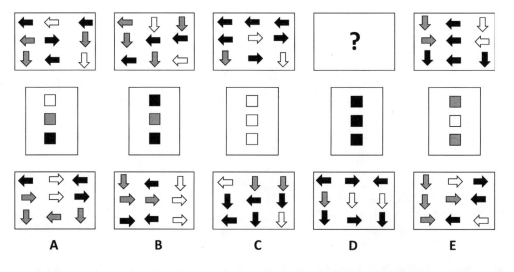

Q27. The middle row of boxes create a rule that has been applied to the boxes directly above them. Which answer option (A to E) corresponds to the rule under the box with the question mark?

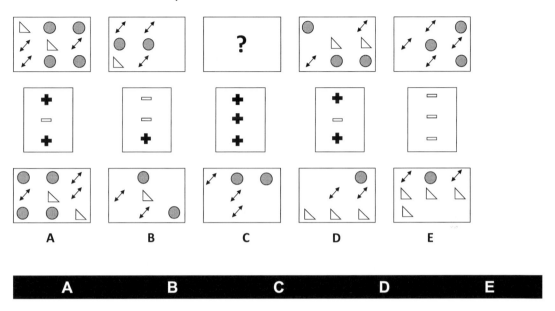

Q28. The middle row of boxes create a rule that has been applied to the boxes directly above them. Which answer option (A to E) corresponds to the rule under the box with the question mark?

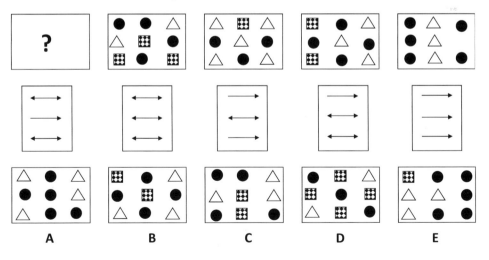

Q29. The middle row of boxes create a rule that has been applied to the boxes directly above them. Which answer option (A to E) corresponds to the rule under the box with the question mark?

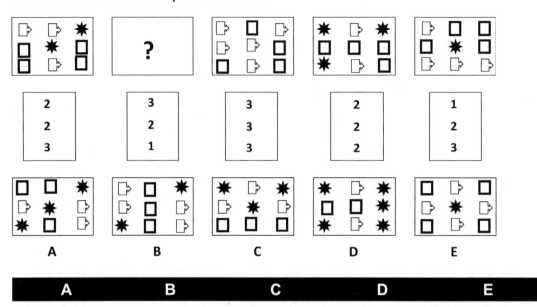

Q30. The middle row of boxes create a rule that has been applied to the boxes directly above them. Which answer option (A to E) corresponds to the rule under the box with the question mark?

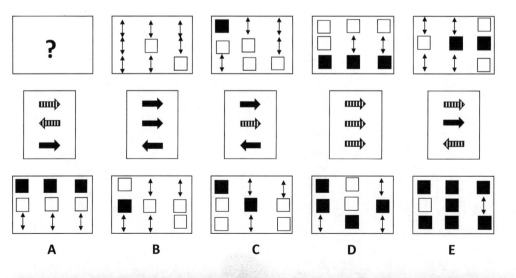

ANSWERS TO NON-VERBAL REASONING – ABSTRACT REASONING

Q1. SET A

The Test Shape fits into Set A because it has two white dots and one black dot. It also has a black square and three squares with diagonal lines through them.

SET A: There are four squares, connected diagonally. Three of these squares are white, with a single diagonal line running through them, and one square is black. Three of these squares has a dot connected to them on their top right-hand corner. Two of the dots are white, whilst one is black. The dot on the square to the left of the black square is always black.

SET B: There are four squares, connected diagonally. All of the squares are white, and three of them have a diagonal line running through them. Each square has a dot connected to its top right-hand corner. Three of these dots are white, and one is black. The black dot is always connected to the square which is left of the square with no diagonal line running through it.

Q2. NEITHER

The Test Shape fits into neither of the two sets. Neither set contains a black square and the Test Shape does. Therefore, it doesn't belong to either set.

SET A: There are four squares in a diagonal line. If a square has no line running through it, then the next square down has a black dot. If the last square in the sequence of four has no line running through it then the first square will have a black dot.

SET B: There are four squares in a diagonal line. If a square has no line running through it, then the second square down from it will have a black dot. If the last square in the sequence of four has no line running through it then the second square from the top will have a black dot.

Q3. SET B

The Test Shape fits Set B because the black dot is two spaces down from the square that has no line running through it. This follows the pattern of Set B.

SET A: There are four squares in a diagonal line. If a square has no line running through it, then the next square down has a black dot. If the last square in the sequence of four has no line running through it then the first square will have a black dot.

SET B: There are four squares in a diagonal line. If a square has no line running through it then, the second square down from it will have a black dot. If the second from last square in the sequence of four has no line running through it, then the first square from the top will have a black dot.

Q4. SET B

The Test Shape fits with Set B because if the square has a diagonal line running through it and a white dot, the next square will have a white dot but no diagonal line in the square. The test shape follows this pattern.

SET A: There are four squares in a diagonal line. If a square has a line running through it and a white dot, then second square down from it also has a white dot but no line running through it. If the last square in the sequence of four is the one with a line running through it and a white dot, then the second square from the top with have a dot but no line running through it.

SET B: There are four squares in a diagonal line. If a square has a line running through it and a white dot then the next one down from it also has a white dot but no line running through it. If the last square in the sequence of four is the one with a line running through it and a white dot, then the first square at the top will have a dot but no line running through it.

Q5. NEITHER

The Test Shape doesn't fit in to either set. In Set A contains three black dots and only one white. Set B contains three white dots and only one black. The Test Shape has four white dots, so therefore cannot fit in to either set.

SET A: There are four black squares in a diagonal line. If a square has a white dot located in the top right-hand corner, then the next square down from it will have a black dot on the bottom left-hand corner. If the last square in the sequence of four is the one with a white dot, then the first square at the top of the sequence will be the one with a black dot on the bottom left-hand corner.

SET B: There are four black squares in a diagonal line. If a square has a black dot located in the top right-hand corner, then the next square down from it will have a white dot on the bottom left-hand corner. If the last square in the sequence of four is the one with a black dot, then the first square at the top of the sequence will be the one with a white dot on the bottom left-hand corner.

Q6. NEITHER

The Test Shape doesn't fit in to either set. In Set A, it contains three black dots. In Set B, it contains three white dots. The Test Shape contains four black dots and therefore cannot fit in to either set.

SET A: There are four black squares in a diagonal line. If a square has no dot located on the top right-hand corner, then the next square down from it will have a black dot on the bottom left-hand corner. If the last square in the sequence of four is the one with no dot, then the first square at the top of the sequence will be the one with a black dot on the bottom left-hand corner.

SET B: There are four black squares in a diagonal line. If a square has no dot located on the top right-hand corner, then the next square down from it will have a white dot on the bottom left-hand corner. If the last square in the sequence of four is the one with no dot, then the first square at the top of the sequence will be the one with a white dot on the bottom left-hand corner.

Q7. NEITHER

The Test Shape doesn't fit in to either set. In Set A, if a shaded square has a dot on the bottom left corner, then the next shaded square will have a dot on the top right corner. In Set B, the same thing is happening as seen in Set A, except they are white dots instead of black. The Test shape shows if the square has a dot on the top right corner, then the next square will have a dot on the bottom left corner.

SET A: There are four black squares in a diagonal line. If a square has a black dot located on the bottom left-hand corner, then the next square down from it will have a black dot on the top right-hand corner. If the last square in the sequence of four is the one with a black dot on the bottom left-hand corner, then the first square at the top of the sequence will be the one with a black dot on the right-hand corner.

SET B: There are four black squares in a diagonal line. If a square has a white dot located on the bottom left-hand corner, then the next square down from it will have a white dot on the top right-hand corner. If the last square in the sequence of four is the one with a white dot in the bottom left-hand corner, then the first square at the top of the sequence will be the one with a white dot in the right-hand corner.

Q8. SET A

The Test Shape fits with Set A. The first vertical square in the sequence means the next square will have an arrow pointing upwards. In the Test Shape, the vertical square is the last in the sequence, so the arrow will be placed at the start of the sequence.

SET A: There are five white squares in a diagonal line. If a square has a vertical line running through it then the next square will have a black arrow pointing upwards. If the last square in the sequence of five is the one with a vertical line running though it then the first square at the top of the sequence will be the one with an arrow pointing upwards.

SET B: There are five white squares in a diagonal line. If a square has an arrow pointing downwards then the second square that follows in the sequence will have a vertical line running through it. If the second to last square in the sequence of five is the one with an arrow pointing downwards then the first square at the top of the sequence will be the one with a vertical line running through it.

Q9. NEITHER

The Test Shapes doesn't fit in to either set. It cannot fit in to Set A because the arrows are pointing up and in the Test Shape, they are pointing down. In Set B, there are four consecutive squares that have horizontal lines, the arrow is placed on the third square. However, the Test Shape places the arrow on the first square that has a horizontal line.

SET A: There are five white squares in a diagonal line. If a square has a vertical line running through it then the next square will have a black arrow pointing upwards. If the last square in the sequence of five is the one with a vertical line running though it then the first square at the top of the sequence will be the one with an arrow pointing upwards.

SET B: There are five white squares in a diagonal line. If a square has an arrow pointing downwards then the second square that follows in the sequence will have a vertical line running through it. If the second to last square in the sequence of five is the one with an arrow pointing downwards then the first square at the top of the sequence will be the one with a vertical line running through it.

Q10. SET B

The Test Shape fits with Set B. If the triangle in the square is pointing to the right, then the next square will have an arrow pointing upwards. It cannot fit into Set A because the arrow is placed above the square that has the triangle pointing to the right.

SET A: There are five white squares in a diagonal line. If a square has an arrow standing on top of it, then the next square in the sequence will have a triangle pointing to the right inside it. If the last square in the sequence of five has an arrow standing on top of it, then the first square in the sequence will be the one with a triangle pointing to the right inside it.

SET B: There are five white squares in a diagonal line. If a square has a triangle pointing to the right inside it, then the next square in the sequence will have an arrow standing on top of it. If the last square in the sequence of five is the one a triangle pointing to the right inside it, then the first square in the sequence will be the one with an arrow standing on top of it.

Q11. B

Within each square the shapes are moving down each line as the sequence progresses. Once they reach the bottom they go back to the top. However, you will notice that each set of shapes alternate colours, switching from black to white and vice versa, as the sequence progresses.

Q12. A

Within each square the shapes are moving round clockwise as the sequence progresses. You will also notice that the square and inner circle which form the centre of each shape are alternating between black and white, as the sequence progresses.

Q13. B

Within each odd numbered square (1 and 3) the shapes are moving round anti-clockwise as the sequence progresses, whilst the central square and circle stay the same colours respectively. Within each even numbered square (2 and 4) the shapes are moving round clockwise as the sequence progresses, whilst the central square and circle stay the same colours respectively.

Q14. NONE

Within each square the shapes are moving round anti-clockwise as the sequence progresses. You will also notice that the square and inner circle, which form the centre of each shape, are each alternating between black and white as the sequence progresses. The diagonal line within each square is moving round clockwise as the sequence progresses.

Q15. B

Within each square the shapes are moving round anti- clockwise as the sequence progresses. You will also notice that the square and inner circle ,which form the centre of each shape, are each alternating between black and white as the sequence progresses. The diagonal line within each square is moving round clockwise as the sequence progresses. The small black dot in the corner of each square is moving round anti-clockwise as the sequence progresses.

Q16. C

Within each square the shapes are all moving round in an anti-clockwise manner as the sequence progresses. The inner circle is alternating between black and chequered as the sequence progresses. The square and small inner circle are alternating between black and white as the sequence progresses. The arrow within each square is spinning clockwise as the sequence progresses.

Q17. D

In the top set of squares, the arrows are moving around the square anti-clockwise one place each time and changing from black to white. The mathematical symbols are moving around the square clockwise one place each time and are changing from white to black. The central rectangular shapes become circular and each section changes from black to white and vice versa.

Q18. A

In the top set of squares the each shape is either the same colour, shade or pattern. For example, arrows pointing down and the multiplication symbols are black, arrows pointing either left or right are white and circles are chequered etc. The only difference between the items in the left square and the right square are that each symbol swaps sides or corner. In the first square, the black arrow pointing downwards in the top left hand corner is now in the bottom right hand corner of the right square etc.

Q19. D

In the top set of squares the rectangle changes from white to black. The triangle changes from black to white and becomes inverted. The thin rectangle goes from white and being in the bottom half to being black and being in the top half.

Q20. D

Within the first set of squares, the shapes in the second square are turned upside down. The top chequered square within the first square is replaced with a chequered circle in the second, and the two squares with internal shapes near the centre alternate between black and white. The number of circles doubles and changes from black to white in the second square.

Q21. A

Within the first set of squares the circles double in number from 5 to 10 and change from white to black. The number of straight lines halves from 8 to 4.

Q22. A

In the top set of squares, the colours and shading of the outer arrows are moving around the square anti-clockwise one place each time. The arrows are also rotating 180 degrees. The colours and shading of the circles are moving around the central axis clockwise one place each time. The central rectangle and inner circle change from white to black and vice versa.

Q23. D

The rule in this question sees the black crosses dictating the number of squares in the pattern above. The rule being applied to box with the question mark means that only one black square should appear in the answer.

Q24. A

The rule in this question sees the grey circles dictating the number of black triangles in the pattern above. The rule being applied to box with the question mark means that two black triangles should appear in the answer.

Q25. E

The rule in this question sees the grey arrows dictating the number of moon shapes in the pattern above. The rule being applied to box with the question mark means that three moon shapes should appear in the answer.

Q26. C

The rule in this question sees the white square dictating the number of arrows pointing to the right in the pattern above. The rule being applied to box with the question mark means that no arrows pointing to the right should appear in the answer.

Q27. D

The rule in this question sees the black plus signs dictating the triangles in the pattern above. The rule being applied to box with the question mark means that three triangles should appear in the answer.

Q28. B

The rule in this question sees the double-sided arrow dictating the number of patterned squares in the pattern above. The rule being applied to box with the question mark means that two patterned squares should appear in the answer.

Q29. E

The rule in this question sees the number '2' dictating the number of sun shapes in the pattern above. The rule being applied to box with the question mark means that one sun shape should appear in the answer.

Q30. C

The rule in this question sees the number of patterned arrows dictating the number of black squares in the pattern above. The rule being applied to box with the question mark means that two black squares should appear in the answer.

Non-Verbal Reasoning – Inductive Reasoning Test

Question 1

Which figure is the odd one out?

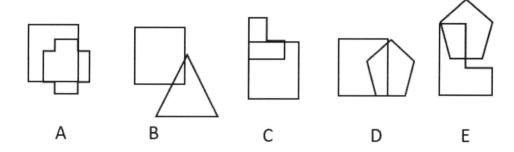

A   B   C   D   E

Answer

Question 2

Which figure fits in with the sequence?

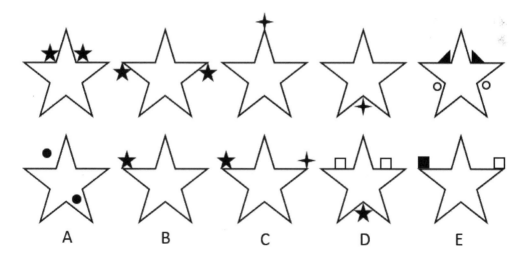

A   B   C   D   E

Answer

Question 3

Which answer fits in with the sequence?

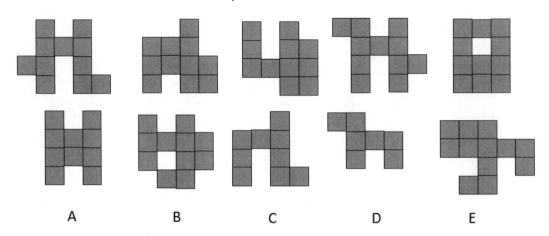

Answer

Question 4

Which figure fits in with the sequence?

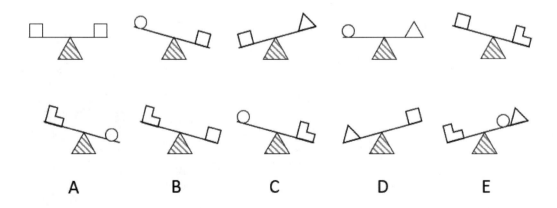

Answer

Question 5

What comes next in the sequence?

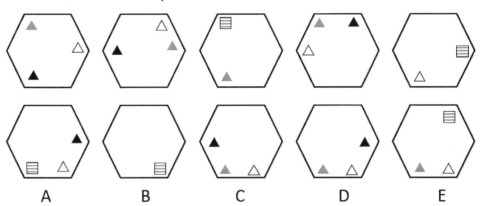

Answer

Question 6

What comes next in the sequence?

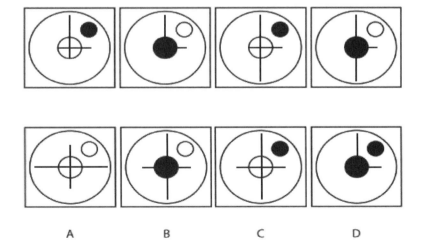

Answer

Question 7

What comes next in the sequence?

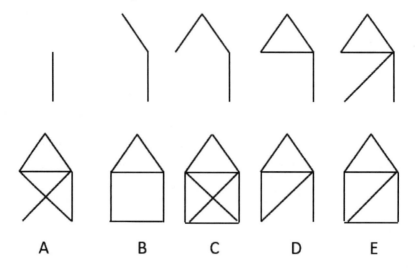

A B C D E

Answer

Question 8

What comes next in the sequence?

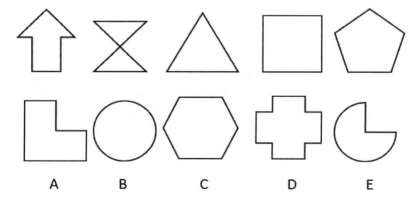

A B C D E

Answer

Question 9

What comes next in the sequence?

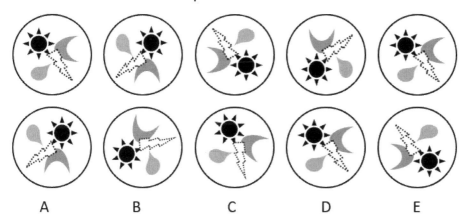

A   B   C   D   E

Answer

Question 10

What comes next in the sequence?

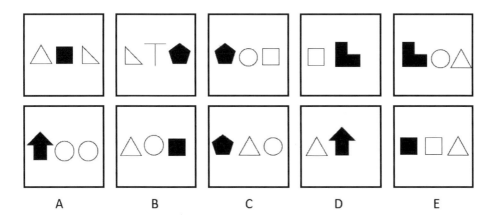

A   B   C   D   E

Answer

Question 11

What comes next in the sequence?

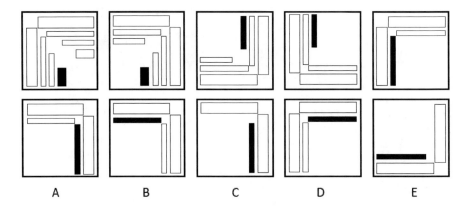

Answer

Question 12

Which answer fits in with the sequence?

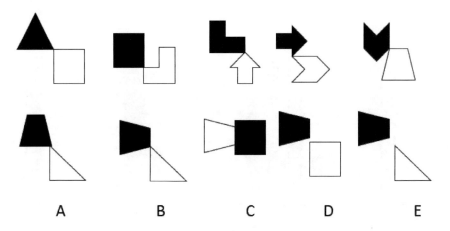

Answer

Question 13

Which answer fits in with the sequence?

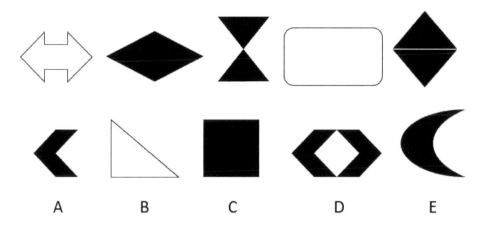

A   B   C   D   E

Answer

Question 14

What comes next in the sequence?

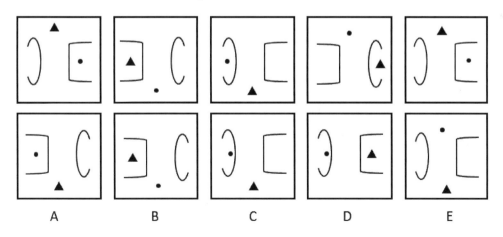

A   B   C   D   E

Answer

Question 15

What comes next in the sequence?

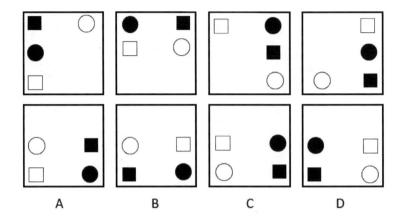

Answer

Question 16

What comes next in the sequence?

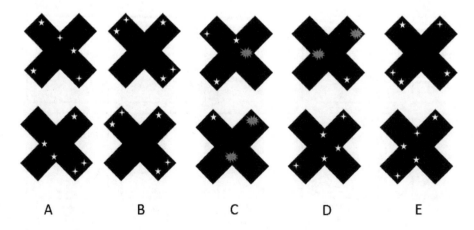

Answer

Question 17

What comes next in the sequence?

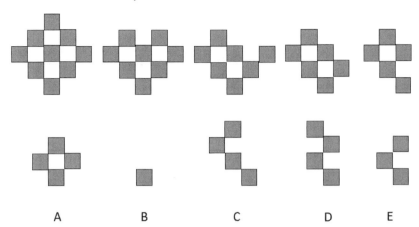

A	B	C	D	E

Answer

Question 18

What comes next in the sequence?

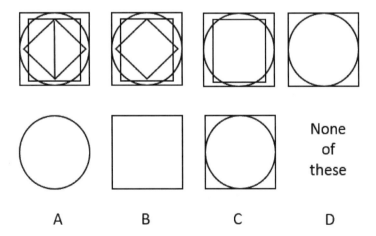

A	B	C	D

Answer

Question 19

What comes next in the sequence?

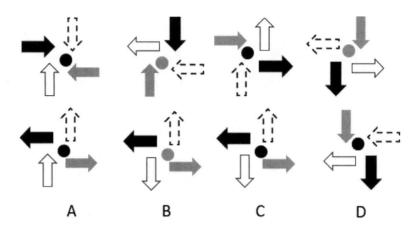

| A | B | C | D |

Answer

Question 20

What comes next in the sequence?

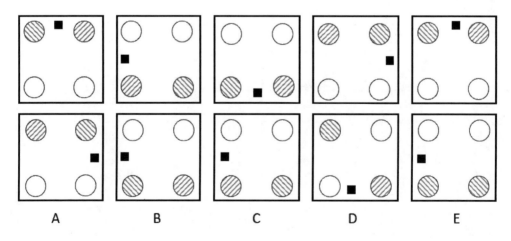

| A | B | C | D | E |

Answer

Question 21

Fill in the missing gap in order to complete the sequence.

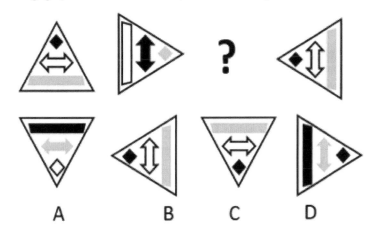

Answer

Question 22

Fill in the missing gap in order to complete the sequence.

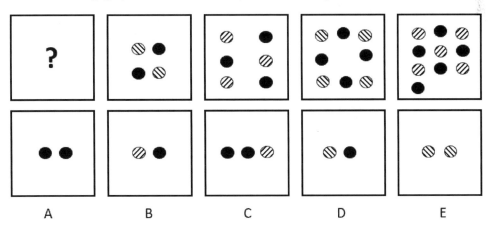

Answer

Question 23

What comes next in the sequence?

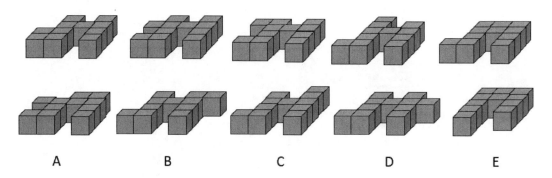

A   B   C   D   E

Answer

Question 24

What comes next in the sequence?

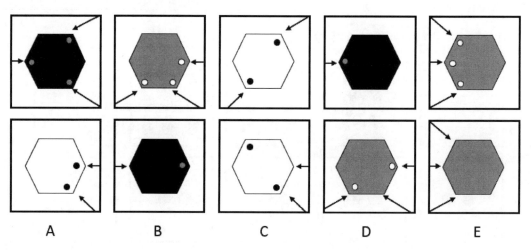

A   B   C   D   E

Answer

Question 25

Fill in the gap in order to complete the sequence.

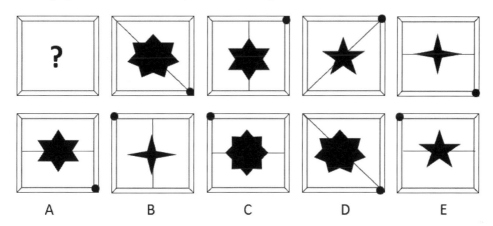

Answer

[ ]

Question 26

Fill in the gap in order to complete the sequence.

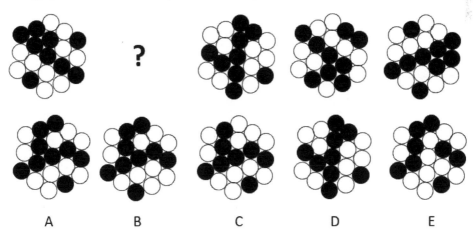

Answer

[ ]

Question 27

Which figure is the odd one out?

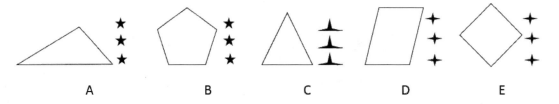

A	B	C	D	E

Answer

Question 28

Which figure is the odd one out?

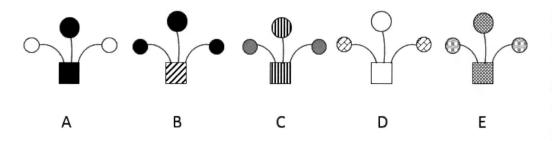

A	B	C	D	E

Answer

Question 29

Fill in the gap in order to complete the sequence.

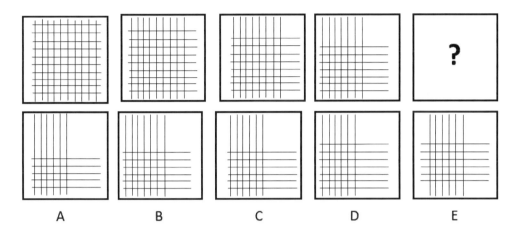

Answer

Question 30

Fill in the gap in order to complete the sequence.

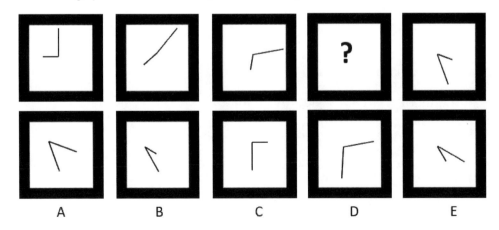

Answer

ANSWERS TO NON-VERBAL REASONING – INDUCTIVE REASONING

Q1. E

Rule 1 = each figure must contain a square.

Figure E is the odd one out because all of the other figures contain a square, whereas Figure E contains an 'L shape' and a Pentagon.

Q2. D

Rule 1 = there must be at least one line of symmetry in the figure.

Figure A can be ruled out because it has no lines of symmetry. Figure B can be ruled out because it has no lines of symmetry. Figure C can be ruled out because the black star on the left would not reflect the black star on the right. Figure E can be ruled out because the black square on the left would not reflect the white square on the right.

Q3. B

Rule 1 = the pattern has to include 11 squares.

Figure A can be ruled out because it only contains 10 squares. Figure C can be ruled out because it only contains 9 squares. Figure D can be ruled out because it only contains 7 squares. Figure E can be ruled out because it contains 12 squares.

Q4. C

Rule 1 = squares weigh more than the circles.

Rule 2 = squares weigh more than the triangles.

Rule 3 = triangles and circles weigh the same.

Rule 3 = 'L' shapes weigh more than the squares.

Figure A can be ruled out because the 'L' shape weighs more than circles, therefore the scales are not correct. Figure B can be ruled out because the 'L' shape weighs more than squares; and therefore the scales are incorrect. Figure D can be ruled out because squares weigh more than triangles. Figure E can be ruled out because you are not given any indication as to whether the circle **and** the triangle together, would weigh less than the 'L' shape.

Q5. D

Rule 1 = the grey triangle moves around the points of the hexagon two places clockwise.

Rule 2 = the white triangle moves around the points of the hexagon one place anti-clockwise.

Rule 3 = the black triangle moves around the points of the hexagon one place clockwise.

Rule 4 = if any of the shapes coincide and end up at the same point, the shapes automatically become a patterned square.

Figure A can be ruled out because a grey square should be positioned in the bottom left corner, and a striped square should be positioned in the bottom right corner. Figure B can be ruled out because a grey triangle needs to be added to the bottom left corner. Figure C can be ruled out because the black triangle should not be there, and the white triangle should be a striped square instead. Figure E can be ruled out because the striped square should be in the position of the white triangle, and the white triangle should be removed.

Q6. C

Rule 1 = the centre circle alternates between white and black.

Rule 2 = the circle in the top right corner alternates between black and white.

Rule 3 = a line is added through the centre of the circle in a clockwise manner (forming a 'plus-like' shape).

Figure A can be ruled out because the white circle in the top right corner needs to be black. Also, the lines horizontally should be shorter than the lines vertically. Figure B can be ruled out because the black centred circle needs to be white. Figure D can be ruled out because the black centred circle needs to be white. Also, a vertical line and a horizontal line need to be added (to form a 'plus-like' shape).

Q7. D

Rule 1 = you need to draw the figure without the pen leaving the paper.

Rule 2 = you cannot go over any line more than once.

Figure A can be ruled out because the next line drawn will be a vertical line to form the left side of the house. Figure B can be ruled out because a diagonal line has disappeared and instead has drawn in the rest of the outer house. Figure C can be ruled out because your next figure will still have 2 lines missing. Figure E can be ruled out because you cannot draw both the bottom line of the house **and** the left horizontal line.

Q8. C

Rule 1 = an extra line of symmetry is added as the sequence progresses.

Figure A can be ruled out because this has no lines of symmetry. Figure B can be ruled out because a circle is symmetrical no matter what way you rotate it. Figure D can be ruled out because this shape has 4 lines of symmetry; we need a shape with 6 lines of symmetry. Figure E can be ruled out because this only has 1 line of symmetry.

Q9. A

Rule 1 = the figure is rotated 90° clockwise as the sequence progresses.

Figure B can be ruled out because it has been rotated approximately 90° anti-clockwise. Figure C can be ruled out because this has been rotated less than 90° clockwise. Figure D can be ruled out because this has been less than 90° rotated (anti-clockwise). Figure E can be ruled out because it has been rotated 180°.

Q10. D

Rule 1 = the first shape in each of the figures, must be the same as the last shape in the previous box.

Rule 2 = the shape with the most number of sides is black.

Rule 3 = all of the sides in each shape must add up to 10.

Figure A can be ruled out because the sides only add up to 9. Figure B can be ruled out because the sides only add up to 8. Figure C can be ruled out because the sides only add up to 9. Figure E can be ruled out because the sides add up to 11. Also, the shape with the most sides is a square; however, there are two squares in this figure, so both squares should be black.

Q11. C

Rule 1 = the figure rotates 90° clockwise as the sequence progresses.

Rule 2 = as the sequence progresses, the black shape switches sides.

Rule 3 = the shaded shape disappears in the next box; and the shape closest to the middle becomes the shaded shape.

Figure A can be ruled out because the small horizontal rectangle should have disappeared. Figure B can be ruled out because the shaded shape should be the small vertical rectangle, not the small horizontal rectangle. Figure D can be ruled out because the figure has been rotated the wrong way, and the black shape should be the vertical rectangle, not the horizontal rectangle. Figure E can be ruled out because the figure has been rotated the wrong way and the shaded rectangle, should be vertical not horizontal.

Q12. B

Rule 1 = the white shape at the end of the figure, becomes a black figure at the start of the next figure.

Rule 2 = the white shape is also rotated 90° clockwise to form the first shape of the next figure.

Rule 3 = both shapes need to be joined at the corner.

Figure A can be ruled out because the black shape has not been rotated 90° clockwise (from the previous figure). Figure C can be ruled out because the trapezoid should be black. Also, the shapes need to be joined at points from both shapes. Figure D can be ruled out because the shapes are not joining by the points of both shapes. Figure E can be ruled out because the shapes are not joining by the points of both shapes.

Q13. D

Rule 1 = each shape needs to contain two lines of symmetry.

Figure A can be ruled out because it only has 1 line of symmetry. Figure B can be ruled out because it has no lines of symmetry. Figure C can be ruled out because it has 4 lines of symmetry. Figure E can be ruled out because it has 1 line of symmetry.

Q14. B

Rule 1 = the two shapes like brackets are rotated 180° each time as the sequence progresses.

Rule 2 = the black dot moves one place around the square in a clockwise manner.

Rule 3 = the black triangle rotates one place around the square in an anti-clockwise manner.

Figure A can be ruled out because the triangle and the dot should be in each other's position. Figure C can be ruled out because the brackets are in the wrong position. The black dot and triangle also need to be in each other's position. Figure D can be ruled out because the brackets are in the wrong position. Also, the black dot should be at the bottom in the middle, and the triangle should be middle left. Figure E can be ruled out because the brackets are in the wrong position. The triangle should be middle left and the black dot should be at the bottom in the middle.

Q15. B

Rule 1 = the shapes move round one place clockwise in each figure.

Figure A can be ruled out because the two squares are in the wrong place; the black square should be where the white square is; and the white square should be where the black square is. Figure C can be ruled out because this is a horizontal reflection of answer option A. Figure D can be ruled out because this is a vertical reflection of answer option C.

Q16. E

Rule 1 = the five pointed stars move around all the points of the cross, two spaces clockwise.

Rule 2 = the four pointed stars move around all the points of the cross, one space anti-clockwise.

Rule 3 = if two or more stars interlink at the same point, the stars become a grey shape.

Figure A can be ruled out because the stars are in the incorrect position. Figure B can be ruled out because it is a replica of box 2. Figure C can be ruled out because none of the stars should overlap at the points. Figure D can be ruled out because the stars are in the incorrect position.

Q17. A

Rule 1 = starting from the top of the figure, and moving around the outer edge of the shape, in a clockwise motion, one square is removed each time.

Figure B can be ruled out because four squares would remain. Figure C can be ruled out because the four squares should form a cross-like shape. Figure D can be ruled out because the four squares should form a cross-like shape. Figure E can be ruled out because the shape should have four squares, not three.

Q18. B

Rule 1 = working from the inside of the shape, outwards, one shape disappears each time.

Figure A can be ruled out because the shape on the outside is a square; and therefore a square would remain. Figure C can be ruled out because this is a replica of box 4. Figure D can be ruled out because one of the answers is correct; so therefore it cannot be 'none'.

Q19. C

Rule 1 = the figure rotates 90° clockwise as the sequence progresses.

Rule 2 = the dot in the centre alternates from black to grey, as the sequence progresses.

Rule 3 = the arrows begin **all** pointing **inwards**. As the sequence progresses, one arrow is turned outwards.

Figure A can be ruled out because the white arrow is pointing inwards; all the arrows should be pointing outwards. Figure B can be ruled out because the grey dot should be a black dot. Figure D can be ruled out because the dashed arrow should be pointing outwards as opposed to inwards.

Q20. C

Rule 1 = the black square rotates 90° anti-clockwise.

Rule 2 = the downward hatching circle follows the pattern of: top left, bottom right, bottom left, top right. The sequence then repeats.

Rule 3 = the upward hatching circle follows the pattern of: top right, bottom left, bottom right, top left. The sequence then repeats.

Q21. A

Rule 1 = the triangle is rotated 90° clockwise as the sequence progresses.

Rule 2 = the shapes inside the triangle remain in the same position; however the colour pattern changes. The colour pattern moves down one space each time, and once it reaches the bottom, it goes back to the top.

Q22. B

Rule 1 = the number of dots increase by 2 each time.

Rule 2 = the diagonal lines alternate from top left to bottom right; to top right to bottom left.

Rule 3 = the number of black dots increases by 1 each time.

Figure A can be ruled out because the first figure should contain one black dot and one striped dot. Figure C can be ruled out because the first figure should contain only two dots, not three. Figure D can be ruled out because the diagonal lines are going the wrong way; they should be top right to bottom left; not top left to bottom right. Figure E can be ruled out because there should be one black dot and one striped dot.

Q23. C

Rule 1 = the first square in the first column moves around the outer edge of the shape one space in a clockwise motion.

Figures A, B, D and E can all be ruled out because the square that is rotating around the outer edge is in the incorrect position for each figure, apart from Figure C.

Q24. A

Rule 1 = the hexagon alternates colour. It changes colour from black, to grey, to white, black-grey-white and so forth.

Rule 2 = the black arrows must be touching the outer squared box.

Rule 3 = the black arrows are used to indicate where the circles should be inside the hexagon.

Rule 4 = the circles inside the shapes follow the colour pattern of: grey, white, black, grey, white, black and so forth.

Figure B can be ruled out because the arrow on the left side of the square, in the middle, should have a circle directly next to it (inside the hexagon); instead the circle is in the middle right corner of the hexagon. Figure C can be ruled out because the circle in the top left corner of the hexagon should be positioned in the middle right corner of the hexagon. Figure D can be ruled out because the middle arrow is pointing to an empty space; either the arrow should be removed or a circle placed where the arrow is pointing. Figure E can be ruled out because there are three arrows, and no circles; the arrows are used to illustrate where the circles should be positioned.

Q25. C

Rule 1 = the black star-shape in the middle of the figure loses one point as the sequence progresses. For example, a six-sided star becomes a five-sided star and then a four-sided star and so on.

Rule 2 = the black dot on the corner of the square rotates clockwise one place, then two places, then three, then four. Once it reaches four it works backwards (anti-clockwise): three spaces, then two, then one and so forth.

Rule 3 = the line in the middle of the shape rotates 45° clockwise, as the sequence progresses.

Figure A can be ruled out because the black star needs to have eight points. Also, the black dot should be in the top left corner. Figure B can be ruled out because the black star needs to have eight points, not four. Also, the vertical line should be horizontal. Figure D can be ruled out because the black star needs to have eight points, not seven. Also, the diagonal line should be horizontal and the black dot should be in the top left corner. Figure E can be ruled out because the five-sided star should be an eight-sided star.

Q26. A

Rule 1 = the dot in the centre remains black throughout the sequence.

Rule 2 = the inner circle (minus the centre circle) moves one space anti-clockwise, as the sequence progresses.

Rule 3 = the outer circles move one space clockwise, as the sequence progresses.

Figure B can be ruled out because the black dot at the bottom centre, should be white, and the black circle should be one space anti-clockwise. Figure C can be ruled out because there should be a black circle at the top centre (outer edge). Figure D can be ruled out because this is an exact replica of figure 3. Figure E can be ruled out because the centred circle should be black, not white.

Q27. A

Rule 1 = the number of points on the large shape should match the number of points on the black star-shape.

Figure A is the odd one out because the large shape contains three points, whereas the number of points on the star-shape is five.

Q28. B

Rule 1 = the shapes opposite each other should be of the same pattern.

Figure B is the odd one out because the pattern in the square (and opposite the black circle) are not of the same colour and pattern. Either the circle should be changed to the same diagonal black and white lines, or the square should be changed to black.

Q29. C

Rule 1 = one line from the top of the horizontal lines is removed as the sequence progresses.

Rule 2 = one line from the far right side of the vertical lines is removed as the sequence progresses.

Figure A can be ruled out because there should be six horizontal lines, not five. Figure B can be ruled out because there should be six vertical lines, not seven. Figure D can be ruled out because there should be six horizontal lines, not seven. Figure E can be ruled out because the lines have been removed from the wrong sides; the horizontal line should be removed from the top, not the bottom; and the vertical line should be removed from the far right side, not the left side.

Q30. E

Rule 1 = the big line moves 40° clockwise as the sequence progresses.

Rule 2 = the small line moves 40° anti-clockwise as the sequence progresses.

Figure A can be ruled out because only one line should be big, the other line should be shorter. Figure B can be ruled out because the short line should be a big line; and the big line should be the short line. Figure C can be ruled out because this is a rotation of the first figure in the sequence. Figure D can be ruled out because neither line is in the correct position.

Numerical Reasoning Explanation

A Numerical Reasoning test is designed to assess mathematical knowledge through number-related assessments. These assessments will consist of different difficulty levels, and will all vary depending on who you are sitting the test for. Be sure to find out what type of Numerical Reasoning test you will be sitting, to ensure you make the most of your preparation time.

Numerical Reasoning tests can be used to assess the following:

Basic Mental Arithmetic	Critical Reasoning	Critical Interpretation	General Intelligence
Estimations	Speed and Concentration	Financial Reasoning	Data Analysis

Below we have provided example numerical questions that *could* be assessed in your assessment. Please note we have provided an array of different types of numerical questions in order to improve your numerical ability. The questions in this guide are NOT an exact replica of the testing questions in your actual assessment – they are merely written as a way of improving your basic numerical understanding.

ADDING FRACTIONS

$$\frac{5}{7} + \frac{3}{5}$$

$$\frac{5}{7} \times \frac{3}{5} = \frac{25 + 21}{35} = \frac{46}{35} = 1\frac{11}{35}$$

Crossbow Method:

The CROSS looks like a multiplication sign and it tells you which numbers to multiply together.

One arm is saying 'multiply the 5 by the 5', and the other arm is saying 'multiply the 7 by the 3'.

The BOW says 'multiply the 2 numbers I am pointing at'. That is 7 times 5.

The answer is 35 and it goes underneath the line in the answer.

SUBTRACTING FRACTIONS

$$\frac{4}{7} - \frac{2}{5}$$

$$\frac{4}{7} \times \frac{2}{5} = \frac{20 - 14}{35} = \frac{6}{35}$$

To subtract fractions, the method is exactly the same. The only difference is, you minus the two numbers forming the top of the fraction, as opposed to adding them.

MULTIPLYING FRACTIONS

$$\frac{2}{3} \times \frac{4}{7}$$

$$\frac{2}{3} \times \frac{4}{7} = \frac{8}{21}$$

Arrow Method:

Multiplying fractions is easy. Draw two arrows through the two top numbers and the two bottom numbers (as shown above) and then multiply – simple!

Sometimes the fraction can be simplified, but in the above example, the answer is already in its simplest form.

Drawing the arrows is just to help you remember which numbers to multiply together. Once you have mastered this knowledge, try doing it without the arrows.

DIVIDING FRACTIONS

$$\frac{3}{7} \div \frac{1}{3}$$

$$\frac{3}{7} \div \frac{3}{1} = \frac{3}{7} \times \frac{3}{1} = \frac{9}{7} = 1\frac{2}{7}$$

Most people think that dividing fractions is difficult. However, it's actually relatively simple if you have mastered multiplying fractions.

Mathematicians realised that if you turn the second fraction upside down (like in the above example), and then change the 'divide' sum to a 'multiply', you will get the correct answer.

SIMPLIFYING FRACTIONS

$$\frac{24}{30} = \frac{12}{15} = \frac{4}{5}$$

Simplifying Fractions

There are a few steps to follow in order to correctly simplify fractions.

*   Can both numbers be divided by 2? If yes, then how many times does 2 go into each number? Write the new fraction.

*   Using the new fraction, do the same thing. Can 2 go into both numbers? If yes, divide both numbers by 2.

*   If both numbers cannot be divided by 2, then try the first odd number: 3. Can both numbers be divided by 3? If yes, divide both numbers by 3. Do this again until 3 no longer goes into the number.

*   If 3 does not go into the numbers again, it doesn't mean it's finished. Try the next odd number: 5, and so on until the fraction can no longer be simplified.

FRACTIONS AND NUMBERS

What is $\dfrac{3}{7}$ of 700?

How to work it out:

- $700 \div 7 \times 3 = 300.$

PERCENTAGES

What is 45% of 500?

How to work it out

- To work out percentages, divide the whole number by 100 and then multiply the percentage you want to find.

- For example:

  - $500 \div 100 \times 45 = 225$

  - So, 225 is 45% of 500.

FRACTIONS / DECIMALS / PERCENTAGES

$$\dfrac{1}{10} = 0.1 = 10\%$$

How to turn fractions into decimals, and decimals into percentages

- 0.1 into a percentage, you would move the decimal point two places to the right, so it becomes 10%.

- To convert $\frac{1}{10}$ into a decimal, you would divide both numbers. For example, $1 \div 10 = 0.1$.

- To convert 10% into a decimal, you move the decimal point two places to the left. For example, to convert 10% into a decimal, the decimal point moves two spaces to the left to become 0.1.

VOLUME

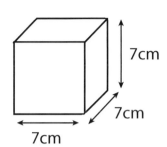

Volume

Length x base x height

- 7 x 7 x 7 = 343

AREAS / PERIMETERS

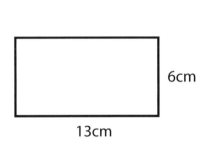

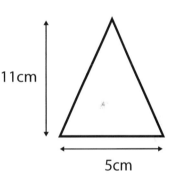

Area of squares / rectangles

Base x height

- 13 × 6 = 78 cm²

Area of triangles

½ base x height

- 11 × 5 ÷ 2 = 27.5

Perimeter

Add all the sizes of each side.

- 6 + 6 + 13 + 13 = 38

TOP TIPS FOR NUMERICAL REASONING!

♦ Make sure you practice your mathematical skills. You will find the numerical reasoning test difficult if you are not great at maths. Practice your adding, subtracting, multiplying and dividing. Also practice mathematics including fractions, percentages and ratios.

♦ Try practising numerical test questions in your head, without writing down your workings out. This is very difficult to accomplish, but it is excellent practice for the real test. Also, practice numerical reasoning tests without a calculator, as you do not want to become completely reliant on the use of a calculator.

♦ If you are permitted to use a calculator, make sure you know how to use one!

♦ Questions will often require you to identify what mathematical formulae is being used (division, percentage, ratio etc.). Before you answer the question, carefully read what the question is asking you! Be sure to understand what you need to work out, before attempting to answer the question.

♦ Practice is key. The more you practice your mental arithmetic and other mathematical formulae; the easier it becomes. This is why we have provided you with lots of sample questions for you to work through. The more you practice these tests, the more likely you are to feel comfortable and confident with the questions. Remember, practice makes perfect!

♦ Make sure you pay attention to detail. Recognising units and measurements and other important mathematical formulas is crucial when it comes to your answer. If a question asks you to write your answer in centimetres, and you write your answer using millimetres, this is a careless mistake that is going to cost you easy marks!

Numerical Reasoning Test

Question 1

A charity arranges a bike race. 120 people take part. ⅓ of the people finish the race in under half an hour. How many people did not finish the race in under half an hour?

Answer

Question 2

What is ⅗ of 700?

Answer

Question 3

There are 4,000 millilitres of water in jugs. If 1 litre is equivalent to 1,000 millilitres, how many litres of water are there?

Answer

Question 4

What is the missing angle?

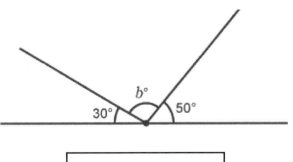

Answer

Question 5

What is 120 multiplied by 13?

Answer

Question 6

Find 60% of £45.

Answer

Question 7

How many lines of symmetry does this shape have?

Answer

Question 8

A packet of biscuits weighs 120 g. Find the weight of 9 packets of biscuits.

A	B	C	D
1080 kg	1880 g	1080 g	108 kg

Question 9

A square field has a perimeter of 72 m. What is the area of the squared field?

Answer

Question 10

What is $^{24}/_{48}$ in its simplest form?

Answer

Question 11

Study the following chart and answer the four questions that follow.

Bike sales

Country	Jan	Feb	Mar	April	May	June	Total
UK	21	28	15	35	31	20	150
Germany	45	48	52	36	41	40	262
France	32	36	33	28	20	31	180
Brazil	42	41	37	32	35	28	215
Spain	22	26	17	30	24	22	141
Italy	33	35	38	28	29	38	201
Total	195	214	192	189	180	179	1149

What percentage of the overall total was sold in April?

A	B	C	D	E
17.8%	17.2%	18.9%	16.4%	21.6%

Question 12

What percentage of the overall total sales were bikes sold to the French importer?

A	B	C	D	E
15.7%	18.2%	18.9%	25.6%	24.5%

Question 13

What is the average number of units per month imported to Brazil over the first 4 months of the year?

A	B	C	D	E
28	24	32	38	40

Question 14

What month saw the biggest increase in total sales from the previous month?

A	B	C	D	E
January	February	March	April	May

Question 15

Study the following chart and answer the four questions that follow.

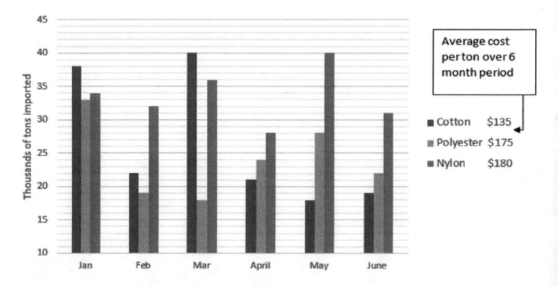

What is the mean value for nylon imported over the 6-month period? (In thousands of tons).

A	B	C	D	E
42.5	18.5	33.5	49.5	37.5

Question 16

What is the range for polyester imports (tons) across the 6-month period?

A	B	C	D	E
15	21	23	52	51

Question 17

What was the difference in thousands of tons between cotton material and nylon material imports in the first 3 months of the year?

A	B	C	D	E
5	15	24	17	2

Question 18

What was the approximate ratio of polyester and nylon material imports in the first 4 months of the year?

A	B	C	D	E
94:120	94:130	92:110	95:100	94:90

Question 19

The lowest percentage for attendance in Year 7 was 51%. The highest attendance was 100%. The median percent for attendance is 70%. The lower quartile percent was 61% and the upper quartile percent was 90%. Represent this information with a box-and-whisker plot.

Question 20

What is the amount of the lower quartile?

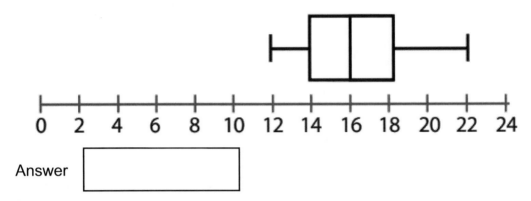

Answer

Question 21

The set of data below shows the results in a year 11 Media mock exam. The marks are out of 100%. The teacher wants to find the mean mark for this test, which was given to 68 pupils. Give your answer to 1 decimal place.

Media mock exam (%)	No. of pupils	No. of pupils X media mock exam (%)
10	0	10 x 0 = 0
20	2	20 x 2 = 40
30	3	
40	6	
50	8	
60	11	
70	8	
80	15	
90	12	
100	3	
Totals	68	

The mean mark is:

Question 22

The two way table shown compares pupils' results for GCSE English with GCSE Media grades.

English GCSE Grades	Media GCSE Grades									Total
	9	8	7	6	5	4	3	2	1	
9										
8		2	2	3						7
7		1	3	4				1		9
6			8	10	6	1				25
5				1		2				3
4								1		1
3										
2										
1										
Total		3	13	18	6	3		2		45

The percentage of pupils who received a Level 5 in Media is approximately what? Give your answer to the nearest whole number.

Answer

Question 23

Below is a stem and leaf diagram showing the finishing time, in seconds, of 15 sprinters who took part in a race.

1	8	9				
2	0	4	5	6	6	9
3	1	3	5	9		
4	0	3	4			
5						

What is the median finishing time?

Answer

Question 24

Using the above stem and leaf diagram, what is the mean finishing time? To one decimal point.

Answer

Question 25

The head of English created the following table, showing the number of pupils in each year group who got a Level 4 or above in their test.

Year Group	No. of pupils	No. of pupils who achieved a Level 4 or above in their English Test
7	86	56
8	93	48
9	102	72
10	99	52
11	106	85
12	68	56

What is the percentage of pupils in all the year groups combined that got a Level 4 or above in their test. Give your answer rounded to a whole number.

Answer

Question 26

Company	Company Profit (Annual) (£)	Cost to buy company (£)	Number of employees
A	15,000	18,000	6
B	26,000	24,000	11
C	22,000	20,000	8
D	40,000	40,000	10

Using the above table, which company has the lowest annual profit per employee?

A	B	C	D	E
Company A	Company B	Company C	Company D	Company C and D

Question 27

Using the above table, approximately how many more employees would company C have to employ to achieve annual profit of £44,000?

A	B	C	D	E
4	11	8	3	19

Question 28

Using the above table, if company A makes an annual profit of £31,000 the following year, what is the percentage increase? Round it up to 1 decimal place.

A	B	C	D	E
106.7%	94.5%	6.6%	51.6%	103.2%

Question 29

Using the above table, if company D makes an annual profit of £15,000 the following year, what is the percentage decrease?

A	B	C	D	E
105.6%	62.5%	33.5%	101.25%	71%

Question 30

Number of pupil absences, from five different classes

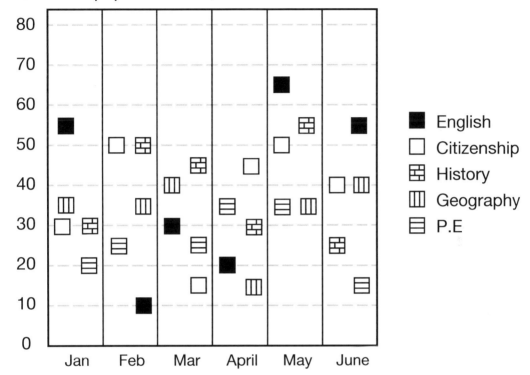

What month saw the mode number of pupils to be absent in the one month period, across all five subjects?

A	B	C	D
February	May	June	March

ANSWERS TO NUMERICAL REASONING TEST

Q1. 80

EXPLANATION = 120 (total number of people) ÷ 3 = 40. This is equal to 1/3. Therefore: 40 x 2 = 80.

Q2. 420

EXPLANATION = 700 ÷ 5 x 3 = 420.

Q3. 4

EXPLANATION = there are 1,000 millilitres in 1 litre. Therefore, 4,000 millilitres is equivalent to 4 litres.

Q4. 100 degrees

EXPLANATION = the angle makes a straight line (which in essence, is a half turn of a circle). Therefore the angles would all need to add up to make 180°. So, 180 – 50 – 30 = 100°.

Q5. 1,560

EXPLANATION = 120 x 13 = 1,560.

Q6. £27

EXPLANATION = £45 ÷ 100 x 60 = £27.

Q7. 0

EXPLANATION = this shape is a parallelogram, and these shapes do not contain a line of symmetry. No matter where you draw the reflection line, the shape cannot be reflected symmetrically.

Q8. C = 1,080 g

EXPLANATION = 120 x 9 = 1,080 g. Pay attention to the measurements; the question is in grams (g), so therefore your answer should also be in grams, unless stated otherwise.

Q9. 324 m²

EXPLANATION = the key thing to remember is that the shape is a square (the sides will be the same length). If the perimeter of the shape is 72 m, then 72 needs to be divided by 4 (4 sides). So, 72 ÷ 4 = 18. Each length of the side is

18 m, and to work out the area = 18 x 18 = 324 m².

Q10. ½

EXPLANATION = $^{24}/_{48}$, both numbers can be divided by 24. 24 goes into 24 once, and goes into 48 twice. Therefore it gives the fraction of ½.

Q11. D = 16.4%

EXPLANATION = to work out the percentage overall total that was sold in April, divide how many bikes were sold in April (189) by the total (1149) and then multiply it by 100. (189 ÷ 1149 x 100 = 16.4).

Q12. A = 15.7%

EXPLANTATION = to work out the overall percentage total that was sold to France, divide how many bikes were sold to France (180) by the total (1149) and then multiply it by 100. (180 ÷ 1149 x 100 = 15.66). Rounded up to 1 decimal place = 15.7.

Q13. D = 38

EXPLANTATION = to work out the average number of units per month imported to Brazil over the first 4 months of the year, you add up the first 4 amounts (Jan-April) and then divide it by how many numbers there are (4). So, (42 + 41 + 37 + 32 = 152 ÷ 4 = 38).

Q14. B = February

EXPLANATION = to find out the biggest increase in total sales from the previous month, you should calculate the difference between the totals for each of the month, and then work out which has the biggest increase. Between January and February, there was an increase by 19. None of the other months have a bigger increase, and therefore February is the correct answer.

Q15. C = 33.5

EXPLANATION = nylon material = 34 + 32 + 36 + 28 + 40 + 31 = 201 ÷ 6 = 33.5.

Q16. A = 15

EXPLANATION = to work out the range, find the smallest and highest number of polyester imports (18) and (33). So, 33 – 18 = 15 (thousands).

Q17. E = 2

EXPLANATION = to work out the difference, add up the first 3 months for cotton (38 + 22 + 40 = 100). Add up the first 3 months for nylon (34 + 32 + 36 = 102). So, the difference between cotton and nylon = 102 – 100 = 2 (thousands).

Q18. B = 94:130

EXPLANATION = 94,000:130,000. Divide both numbers by 1000 to give you 94:130.

Q19. Your box and whisper plot diagram should look like this:

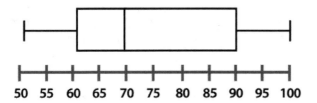

Q20. 14

EXPLANATION = the lower quartile range is the first line that forms the box. So, the correct answer would be 14.

Q21. 67.2%

EXPLANATION = add up the "number of pupils multiplied by media mock exam" and then divide it by the "number of pupils".

Media mock exam (%)	No. of pupils	No of pupils X media mock exam (%)
10	0	10 X 0 = 0
20	2	20 X 2 = 40
30	3	30 X 3 = 90
40	6	40 X 6 = 240
50	8	50 X 8 = 400
60	11	60 X 11 = 660
70	8	70 X 8 = 560
80	15	80 X 15 = 1200
90	12	90 X 12 = 1080
100	3	100 X 3 = 300
Totals		

So, 4570 ÷ 68 = 67.2%.

Q22. 13%

EXPLANATION = number of pupils who received a D grade in Media = 6.

Total number of pupils = 45.

So, 6 ÷ 45 x 100 = 13.333%. To the nearest whole number = 13%.

Q23. 29 seconds

EXPLANATION = 'median' simply means 'middle'. So, what number is in the middle? Using the data in ascending order, you will notice that 29 (seconds) is the median/middle number.

Q24. 30.1 seconds

EXPLANATION = to work out the mean number, add up all the numbers and then divide it by how many numbers there are.

So, 452 ÷ 15 = 30.133. To one decimal point = 30.1.

Q25. 67%

EXPLANATION = add up total number of pupils = 554.

Add up the number of pupils who achieved a C grade or above in English = 369.

To work out the overall percentage = 369 ÷ 554 x 100 = 66.6%.

To the nearest whole number = 67%.

Q26. B = Company B

EXPLANATION = simply divide the annual profit for each company by the number of employees, and see which company has the lowest profits.

Q27. C = 8

EXPLANATION = 44,000 ÷ 2750 = 16. That is 8 more than what they have already.

Q28. A = 106.7%

EXPLANATION = 31,000 – 15,000 = 16,000.

So, 16,000 ÷ 15,000 x 100 = 106.666% = 106.7%

Q29. B = 62.5%

EXPLANATION = 40,000 − 15,000 = 25,000.

So, 25,000 ÷ 40,000 x 100 = 62.5%.

Q30. B = May

EXPLANATION = you need to add up all of the subjects for each month. January = 170, February = 170, March = 155, April = 145, May = 240, June = 175. Therefore the mode (the most) in one given month is in May.

Writing Tests

Of course, being able to accurately relay information in writing is an extremely important skill for a Police Officer. As you will have seen earlier, each state has slightly different method of testing that applicants have this ability to a sufficient standard. As a result, we have created this generic report writing exercise which will allow you to practise your summary writing and extended writing skills. Continue below for the instructions and exercises.

Report Writing Exercises

Read and study the following sample report writing exercise before following the guidance on how to answer it.

You are the customer services officer for a fictitious retail centre. Your manager has asked you to compile a report based on a new pub that is being opened in the centre. Your manager is meeting with the pub owners in a few days' time to discuss a few issues and he wants you to write a report based on the information provided. The pub owners have requested that the pub is open to serve alcohol beverages in the centre from 11am until 11pm.

At the bottom of this page there is a survey sheet that tells you that, on the whole, the general public and staff are not happy with the idea of a pub being opened in the shopping centre because of perceived antisocial behavioural problems, littering and rowdiness.

It is your job to create a report for your manager stating what the main issues are and what your recommendations would be.

SURVEY SHEET

The following information has been taken from a survey that was conducted amongst 100 members of public who regularly shop at the centre and 30 employees who work at the centre.

- 60% of the general public and 80% of employees felt that the opening of a pub in the centre would increase littering.

- 80% of the general public and 60% of employees thought that rowdiness in the centre would increase as a result of the pub opening.

- 10% of the general public and 10% of employees thought that the opening of the pub would be a good idea.

Below, there is an example of how the report could be written. There are many different recommendations that could have been made. You should consider the information you have gathered and make the recommendation(s) you consider to be the best for those circumstances.

Remember: recommendations are suggestions for actions or changes.

They should be specific rather than general. It is important that you answer the question and state what your main findings and recommendations are.

SAMPLE RESPONSE TO WRITTEN EXERCISE

From: The Customer Services Officer

To: The Centre Manager

Subject: New pub

Sir,

Please find detailed my findings and recommendations in relation to the new pub as requested. The survey conducted took into the consideration the views and opinions of 100 members of the public and 30 members of staff who work at the centre.

Whilst a small proportion of staff and public (10%) felt that the opening of the pub would be a good idea, the majority of people surveyed felt that there would be problems with anti-social behaviour, littering and rowdiness.

Having taken into consideration all of the information provided, I wish to make the following recommendations:

The level of customer service that the centre currently provides is high and it is important that this is maintained. It is important to take into consideration the views and opinions of our customers and staff and to see things from their point of view. I believe that there would be a high risk involved if we were to allow the pub to serve alcoholic beverages from 11am until 11pm and that problems with anti-social behaviour could develop. We have a responsibility to protect the public and to ensure that they are safe whilst in the centre.

Whilst it is important to initially obtain the views of the pub owners, I recommend that the pub is only permitted to serve alcoholic beverages from 11am until 1pm and from 5pm until 7pm so as to reduce the risk of the above problems developing.

I have recommended this course of action, as I believe it is in the best interests of the centre, its staff and more importantly our valued customers. This alternative course of action would be for a trial period only and providing there are no problems with anti-social behaviour, littering or rowdiness we could look to review the opening hours with a view to extending them. I am prepared to take full responsibility for monitoring the situation once the pub has been opened. I will keep you updated on progress.

The Customer Services Officer

How to create an effective report – the 5-step approach

Now that you have read the sample response, look at the following 5-step approach that you should use when creating a well-structured report.

Step 1 – Read the information provided in the exercise quickly and accurately.

Remember that you only have 20 minutes in which to create your report. Therefore, you do not want to spend too long reading the information. We would suggest that you spend 2-3 minutes reading the information.

Step 2 – Extract relevant information from irrelevant information (main findings).

When you read the information provided in the exercise, you will notice that some of the information is of no significance. Write down which information is relevant in brief details only – these should be your main findings.

Step 3 – Decide what recommendations you are going to suggest or what action(s) you are going to take.

One of the police officer core competencies is that of problem solving. If asked to, then you must come up with suitable recommendations. Do not 'sit on the fence', but rather provide a logical solution to the problem.

Step 4 – Construct your report in a logical and concise manner.

You are being assessed on your ability to communicate effectively. Therefore, you must construct your report in a logical and concise manner. You must also ensure that you answer the question.

Step 5 – Include keywords and phrases from the core competencies in your report.

During each report or letter that you construct we strongly advise that you include keywords and phrases from the core competencies.

You will notice that the 5-step approach is easy to follow. Therefore, I strongly suggest that you learn it and use it during the practise exercises that now follow. You have 20 minutes to complete each individual exercise.

WRITTEN REPORT EXERCISE 1

You are the customer services officer for a fictitious retail centre. Your manager has asked you to compile a report regarding a number of complaints he has received from shop owners who state that rowdy youths are intimidating shop owners at the centre which is having a detrimental effect on their business generally and more importantly their takings. Visitor numbers at the centre are down 25% over the last 3 months.

CCTV reports suggest that a gang of 8 youths have been circling the centre during daylight shopping hours, often approaching customers and harassing them for spare change.

The editor of a local newspaper has become aware of these incidents and is sending a reporter along to interview your manager to see what the main problems are and what the centre intends to do about them.

Your report should detail your main findings as well as your recommendations as to how the situation can be resolved.

Write your response in the form of a letter to your manager, which you are writing to advise him on the situation before his interview.

WRITTEN REPORT EXERCISE 2

You are the customer services officer for a fictitious retail centre. Your manager has received a request from the local council Anti-Truancy Group who wish to patrol the centre in groups of 6 people for five-day period next month.

During their request the Anti-Truancy Group has raised concerns that schoolchildren from the local area are congregating at the retail centre during school hours. CCTV cameras have confirmed these reports.

Local police have also confirmed in a recent report that anti-social behaviour in and around the retail centre has increased by 15% in the last four weeks alone.

You are to create a report for your manager that details your main findings and your recommendations.

WRITTEN REPORT EXERCISE 3

You are the customer services officer for a fictitious retail centre. During a recent fire safety inspection at the retail centre, local Fire Officers found a large number of fire escapes blocked with cardboard boxes that had been stored by shop owners. They also noticed that many of the general areas were untidy and the housekeeping was below an acceptable standard.

Whilst the obstructions were removed at the time of the inspection, and the Fire Service will not be taking any further action, your manager is concerned that this type of incident will happen again.

He has asked you to create a report detailing your recommendations as to how this type of incident can be prevented in the future and also how the standard of housekeeping can be improved.

Create your response in the form of a letter to your manager.

WRITTEN REPORT EXERCISE 4

As the customer services officer for a fictitious retail centre you are required to provide your manager with a written report based on the following information.

Currently at the centre there are 3 unoccupied shops. A local charity would like to use one of the shops for a 3-month period free of charge in order to raise money for charity by selling second hand clothes and goods.

Your manager has already conducted a survey of all shop owners and staff at the centre to see what they feel about the proposal and the results are as follows:

- 15% of shop owners support the idea;

- 5% of shop owners do not have an opinion;

- 80% of shop owners are against the idea;

- 90% of staff at the centre support the idea.

You are to create a report detailing your main findings and recommendations based on the information provided.

WRITTEN REPORT EXERCISE 5

You are the customer services officer for a fictitious retail centre. Over the last 4 weeks the retail centre has been extremely busy and trade has been excellent. However, an issue has arisen whereby car owners are complaining that there are not enough car park spaces at the centre.

Many of the shop owners are complaining that they are losing trade as many potential customers are turning their backs on the centre during busy periods due to the lack of car parking spaces.

A petition has been signed by every shop owner at the centre supporting the removal of the disabled car parking spaces and reallocating them as standard car parking spaces in order to resolve the problem. There are currently 200 car parking spaces allocated at the centre specifically for disabled badge users.

Your manager is meeting with the shop owners in two days' time to discuss their proposal. He wants you to create a report detailing the key issues and your recommendations.

Cognitive Tests

Cognitive tests are an important element of a psychometric test. The tests are designed to measure trait intelligence (IQ) and cognitive ability, which is indicated by your efficiency in information processing. Whilst IQ and aptitude tests are designed to test your intelligence, you can actually practice for them, which in turn has been proven to increase scores.

In the majority of cognitive tests, you are not expected to answer all of the questions. When you turn over the test paper, or when you start your online test, you may see that the total number of questions in the test is excessive for the amount of time you are given to answer them. If this is the case, do not panic; you are not expected to finish the test. Test tests are usually designed so that it is very difficult to complete all of the questions. The key to remember is that you must try to answer as many questions as possible, but you should also aim for accuracy. Some test centres will deduct marks of incorrect answers or guessing; therefore, the key to passing the tests is to aim for speed as well as accuracy!

A few commonly asked questions to do with cognitive tests:

Why do most people fail the tests?

One of the more common reasons why people fail their test is because they do not read the question. It is vitally important you read the questions carefully, and also take the time to listen to the brief, prior to the test.

You should pay particular attention to how you are required to answer the questions. Are you required to circle the right answer, strike it through, shade a box of your answer option, or write your answer option on a separate answer book? Don't forget, if you pass a question you must make sure you leave a gap on the answer sheet, otherwise ALL of your proceeding answers will be wrong!

It is a good idea to pay attention to the time limit for the test. For example, if there are 40 questions in the test and you have 10 minutes to complete them, this gives you just 15 seconds per question on average. If you get stuck on a particular question, move on and come back to it later if you have time, but don't forget to leave a space on the answer sheet.

Is it acceptable for me to guess an answer, if I find that I am running out of time?

Our advice is to avoid wild-guessing at all costs! Remember, some test centres will deduct marks for incorrect answers. Having said that, it is certainly worth learning the skill of what is called 'best-guessing'. Best-guessing can only be utilised during multiple-choice type questions. It basically requires you to eliminate quickly any glaringly incorrect answer options. This technique is a useful one if you find that you are short of time and have not answered enough questions to gain high marks. For example if you can easily see that an answer should be within a specific range, or it needs to have certain units, you should be able to discount two or three of the answer options quickly, which then leaves you with a 50:50 chance of getting the answer correct.

Are there any further tips you can offer me to help me prepare fully for my tests?

- Whilst it is important to find out the types of questions you will be required to undertake during the real test, variety during practice will help you to increase your scores. We recommend that you attempt a variety of different test questions, such as general psychometric tests, numerical reasoning, verbal reasoning, abstract reasoning, spatial aptitude, fault analysis and mechanical reasoning etc. This will undoubtedly improve your overall ability to pass the IQ and aptitude test that you are required to undertake. If you go to **www.PsychometricTestsOnline.co.uk** then you will be able to try all of these free of charge.

- Confidence is an important part of test preparation. Have you ever sat a timed test, and had your mind go blank? This is because your mind is focused on negative thoughts and your belief that you will fail the test. If you practice plenty of test questions under timed conditions then your confidence will grow. If your confidence is at its peak at the commencement of the test then there is no doubt that you will actually look forward to sitting it, as opposed to being fearful of the outcome.

- Whilst this is a very basic tip that may appear obvious, many people neglect to follow it. Make sure that you get a good night's sleep the night before your test or assessment. Research has shown that those people who have regular 'good' sleep are far more likely to concentrate better during IQ and aptitude tests.

- Aim for SPEED as well as ACCURACY. Many test centres want to see how quickly you can work, but they also want to see how accurate your work is, too. Therefore, when tackling the tests you must work as quickly as you can without sacrificing accuracy. Most tests are designed so that you do no finish them and you will most probably lose marks for incorrect answers.

- You are what you eat! In the week prior to the test eat and drink healthily. Avoid cigarettes, alcohol and food with high fat content. The reason for this is that all of these will make you feel sluggish and you will not perform at your peak. On the morning of your assessment eat a healthy breakfast such as porridge and a banana.

- Drink plenty of water, always!

- If you have any special needs that need to be catered for ensure you inform the assessment centre staff prior to the assessment day. You will not be treated negatively; in fact the exact opposite. They will give you extra time in the tests which can only work in your favour.

Now we have provided you with a number of important tips, take the time to work through the nine different sample test sections that are contained within the guide.

You will need a stopwatch in order to assess your performance against the time constraints for each test.

With regards to using a calculator during the sample tests, please try to tackle them without one, as this will help to improve your confidence and ability during the real test.

COGNITIVE TEST SECTION 1

(Mental arithmetic)

In this section there are 50 questions and you have just 20 minutes to answer them.

COGNITIVE TEST SECTION 1

Q1. What is 8 multiplied by 6?

Answer

Q2. What is 4 multiplied by 7?

Answer

Q3. What is 6 multiplied by 9?

Answer

Q4. What is 9 multiplied by 9?

Answer

Q5. What is 8 multiplied by 7?

Answer

Q6. What is 12 multiplied by 6?

Answer

Q7. What is 13 multiplied by 7?

Answer

Q8. What is 12 multiplied by 12?

Answer

Q9. What is 15 multiplied by 6?

Answer

Q10. What is 20 multiplied by 20?

Answer

Q11. What is 50% of 250?

Answer

Q12. What is 60% of 500?

Answer

Q13. What is 40% of 300?

Answer

Q14. What is 70% of 800?

Answer [   ]

Q15. What is 45% of 120?

Answer [   ]

Q16. What is 65% of 210?

Answer [   ]

Q17. What is 32% of 98, to one decimal place?

Answer [   ]

Q18. What is 44% of 200?

Answer [   ]

Q19. What is 56% of 170?

Answer [   ]

Q20. What is 80% of 900?

Answer [   ]

Q21. What is $\frac{4}{5}$ of 70?

Answer

Q22. What is $\frac{3}{4}$ of 180?

Answer

Q23. What is $\frac{2}{6}$ of 300?

Answer

Q24. What is $\frac{5}{8}$ of 64?

Answer

Q25. What is $\frac{7}{8}$ of 136?

Answer

Q26. What is $\frac{9}{13}$ of 208?

Answer

Q27. What is $\frac{1}{4}$ of 800?

Answer

Q28. What is ⅔ of 660?

Answer

Q29. What is 4⁄7 of 154?

Answer

Q30. What is ⅖ of 412?

Answer

Q31. Multiply 11 by 5 and then divide by 5

Answer

Q32. Multiply 6 by 7 and then divide by 3

Answer

Q33. Multiply 8 by 9 and then divide it by 2

Answer

Q34. Divide 24 by 3 and then multiply it by 4

Answer

Q35. Divide 49 by 7 and then multiply it by 12

Answer

Q36. Subtract 12 from 84 and then divide it by 4

Answer

Q37. Subtract 14 from 92 and then multiply it by 2

Answer

Q38. Multiply 6 by 4 and then divide it by 3

Answer

Q39. Divide 56 by 7 and then subtract it by 5

Answer

Q40. Multiply 6 by 6 and then multiply it by 4

Answer

Q41. What is 13 multiplied by 3?

Answer

Q42. What is 15 multiplied by 5?

Answer

Q43. What is 20 multiplied by 120?

Answer

Q44. What is 30% of 400?

Answer

Q45. What is 5% of 150?

Answer

Q46. What is 95% of 60?

Answer

Q47. What is $\frac{9}{11}$ of 88?

Answer

Q48. What is $\frac{2}{7}$ of 490?

Answer

Q49. Multiply 8 by 3 and then multiply it by 3

Answer ☐

Q50. Divide 120 by 4 and then multiply it by 5

Answer ☐

Please now check your answers carefully before moving onto the next section of the guide.

ANSWERS TO COGNITIVE TEST SECTION 1

Q1. 48	Q25. 119	Q49. 72
Q2. 28	Q26. 144	Q50. 150
Q3. 54	Q27. 200	
Q4. 81	Q28. 440	
Q5. 56	Q29. 88	
Q6. 72	Q30. 164.8	
Q7. 91	Q31. 11	
Q8. 144	Q32. 14	
Q9. 90	Q33. 36	
Q10. 400	Q34. 32	
Q11. 125	Q35. 84	
Q12. 300	Q36. 18	
Q13. 120	Q37. 156	
Q14. 560	Q38. 8	
Q15. 54	Q39. 3	
Q16. 136.5	Q40. 144	
Q17. 31.4	Q41. 39	
Q18. 88	Q42. 75	
Q19. 95.2	Q43. 2400	
Q20. 720	Q44. 120	
Q21. 56	Q45. 7.5	
Q22. 135	Q46. 57	
Q23. 100	Q47. 72	
Q24. 40	Q48. 140	

COGNITIVE TEST SECTION 2

(Abstract and Diagrammatic Reasoning)

The time limit for each part is indicated at the beginning of the test.

COGNITIVE TEST SECTION 2

You have 10 minutes to complete this section.

Q1. Which SET does the TEST SHAPE belong to?

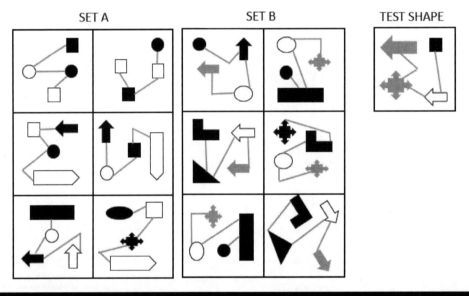

A	B	C
Set A	Set B	Neither

Q2. Which SET does the TEST SHAPE belong to?

SET A	SET B	TEST SHAPE

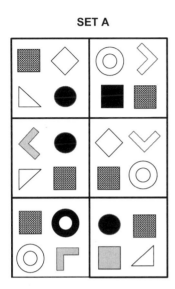 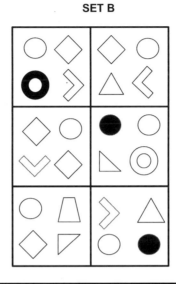 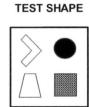

A	B	C
Set A	Set B	Neither

Q3. Which SET does the TEST SHAPE belong to?

SET A	SET B	TEST SHAPE

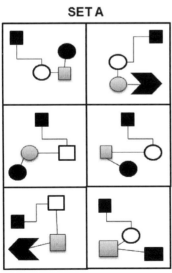 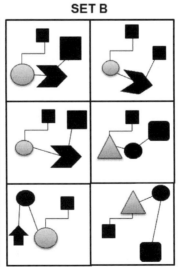 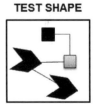

A	B	C
Set A	Set B	Neither

Q4. Which SET does the TEST SHAPE belong to?

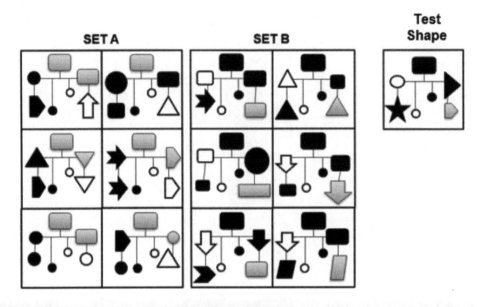

A	B	C
Set A	Set B	Neither

Q5. Which SET does the TEST SHAPE belong to?

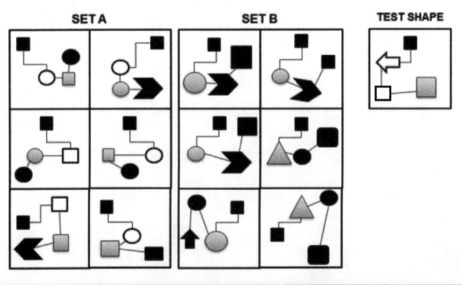

A	B	C
Set A	Set B	Neither

ANSWERS TO COGNITIVE TEST (PART 2)

Q1. Neither

Explanation: The test shape does not fit in to either Sets. It does not fit in to either sets because the test shape has two grey shapes, which does not follow the pattern in either set.

Q2. Set A

Explanation: The test shape fits in to Set A. This is because in set A each square contains a black shape, a white shape, a chequered shape and a grey shape. This is apparent in the Test shape and therefore belongs to this set.

Q3. Set B

Explanation: The test shape fits in to Set B. Set B starts with a black shape, which is linked to a grey shape, to a black shape, to a black shape. The Test shape follows this pattern and therefore belongs to this set.

Q4. Set B

Explanation: The test shape fits in to set B. Set B starts with a black shape. The row below then follows the sequence white and black. The bottom line follows the sequence black, white, black and grey. Therefore the test shape follows set B.

Q5. Neither

Explanation: The test shape does not belong to either Sets. It is clear that the test shape contains two white shapes. Neither of the sets follows this pattern and therefore cannot belong to either set.

Comprehension Tests

Essentially, comprehension tests assess your ability to do the following:

*   Read text and identify key points;

*   Distinguish fact from opinion;

*   Understand content to a degree which allows you to summarise it in your own words;

*   Make inferences and deductions based on the information given;

*   Identify readership and/or rewrite information for a different target audience;

*   Evaluate which points are more important than others;

*   Assess contradictions, implied statements and support statements.

Comprehension Tips

When answering the comprehension section of the test, make sure to read the entire text closely. You should read through the entire text before looking at the questions so that you can understand the overall tone and context of the passage. After reading through it once, take a look at the questions and then re-read the text, bearing the questions in mind.

Comprehension – Sample Questions

The text will be used for all sample questions in this chapter. Make sure to read through the whole passage first before attempting any questions.

The following text is an article from a fictional education journal:

The school have opted to introduce the "20th Century Awareness Project", starting with the "First World War Awareness Programme". The aim of these two projects is to strengthen younger students' understanding of the events of the 20th century.

The school's leadership team believed it was necessary to better teach the history of the 20th century to all students, particularly the period of 1900-1918. This was due to concerns that younger pupils would not naturally be exposed to the First World War in a sensitive manner, and that depictions of it in popular culture (e.g. film, video-games, television programmes) might not convey the horrors of the war enough, instead choosing to glorify conflict as a whole.

Mrs. Brown, the school's head teacher, claimed that the First World War was "the most important event in recent history" as it shaped the modern world. To an extent, Mrs. Brown's statement is correct. The League of Nations was founded in 1920 mostly as a response to the events of the First World War, which in turn set a precedent for multinational legislative bodies such as the European Union and the United Nations. Additionally, Germany's defeat in the war and subsequent reparation expenses arguably resulted in the rise of the Nazi party and therefore the Second World War, which would shape the world even further.

Mrs. Brown continued, expressing concern that younger pupils might not be learning about the war outside of school. She argued that if we fail to pass on our understanding of such terrible events to younger generations, people in the future won't know the lessons that we've learnt from history.

The school's decision to create a greater focus on the First World War in both history lessons and PSHE (Personal Social Health Education) classes was received well by most teachers as well as a number of students. Teachers have opted to keep the teaching of the First World War interesting by using roleplays and documentaries.

As part of this initiative, the school has decided to devote four assemblies each year to 20th Century history to supplement the focus in lessons. The goal was to provide context to the First World War by discussing events which preceded and followed it. While they were received less favourably than the lessons, these sessions could be more light-hearted and therefore counterbalanced the sombre tone of the First World War lessons.

The final part of the initiative was to promote the teaching of the war and 20th Century history outside of school, with Mrs. Brown urging parents and guardians to visit important historical sites with their children. "By taking our young people to places such as Ypres, we can ensure that they fully understand the cost of war, and make sure that major conflicts like the First and Second world wars never happen again."

Moving forward, the school hopes that these initiatives will do the following:

- Increase the number of students interested in studying History at A-level and university;

- Make students more aware of good and bad depictions of the war in popular culture;

- Make PSHE a more credible lesson in the school;

- Inspire other schools to follow suit and create a stronger focus on 20th Century history.

Presenting the Main Points of a Text

Questions of this kind will ask you to choose from a selection of statements, which match the main points of a text. In the test, you will have to pick four statements and drag them into empty boxes.

Teachers and students approved of the new lesson focus.
Parents/guardians should make their children aware of the First World War.
The school has decided to create a larger focus on 20th Century history.
The assemblies weren't as well-received as the lessons.
Young students might not be exposed to the history of the war in a sensitive manner.
The First World War is one of the most important events in recent history.
The goal of the assemblies was to provide context to the history lessons.
If we fail to pass our information to future generations, the lessons we've learnt won't carry over either.
The assemblies were more light-hearted than the lessons.

Matching the Content of the Text to a Summary

For this kind of question, you will be asked to refer to certain paragraphs from the text, and then choose a summary from the selection of answers which matches it best.

Refer to paragraphs 4 and 5. Which of these summaries best suits them?

☐ Young pupils need to learn about the war outside of school.

☐ Teachers have opted to use documentaries and roleplays to keep the new classes interesting.

☐ The head teacher was concerned that students were not learning enough about the First World War outside of school. The new classes focus on it were received well.

❏ Parents/guardians should assist in teaching their children about 20th Century history.

Highlighting the Meaning of Words and Phrases

Questions of this kind will usually highlight part of a sentence from the paragraph, and then ask you to choose from a list of alternative phrases. By doing this, you are showing that you understand the meanings of the words used in the text, since you can substitute them for different phrases.

Re-read the following phrase from paragraph 6 and choose the phrase which is closest to it in meaning.

"… and therefore counterbalanced the sombre tone of the First World War lessons."

❏ … And therefore reduced the sombre tone…

❏ … And therefore compensated for the sombre tone…

❏ … And therefore added to the sombre tone…

❏ … And therefore had overridden the sombre tone…

Sequencing Information from the Text

This type of question expects you to choose statements which represent the order of information in the passage. This could be a sequence of steps written in the text, or the sequence of information given.

For this question, list the three steps in the school's initiative to increase awareness of 20th Century history. Mark them as "FIRST" "SECOND" and "THIRD".

❏ Create a focus on 20th Century history in all lessons.

❏ Create a focus on the First World War in History and PSHE lessons.

❏ Take students on school trips to important historical sites.

❏ Encourage parents/guardians to teach their children about 20th Century history.

❑ Promote elements of popular culture which depict the First World War in a positive light.

❑ Devote assemblies to discussion about 20th Century history.

❑ Create a focus on 20th Century history in all History classes.

Completing a List based on the Content of the Text

When attempting this type of question, you will need to choose statements which complete a list of bullet points found in the passage. For this question, the third point has been filled in for you.

-

-

-   Make PSHE a more credible lesson in the school.

-

❑ Urge parents to get involved in the teaching of their children.

❑ Decrease focus on the Middle Ages in History lessons.

❑ Increase awareness for different kinds of depiction about the war.

❑ Make assemblies more interesting.

❑ Be an example to other schools.

❑ Encourage more students to study history.

❑ Reduce troublemakers in lessons.

Attributing Statements to Elements of the Text

This type of question involves elements of the text (often categories) which must be matched with a selection of statements. For this example, write the number in the box. For the actual test, you will need to drag an abbreviation for the element into the box next to the statement.

Read the following statements and decide which refer to:

1. The League of Nations

2. The 20th Century Awareness Project

3. The First World War Awareness Programme

4. PSHE

❒ A project with the aim of changing the school's overall focus regarding history.

❒ Personal Social Health Education.

❒ A project devoted to changing the focus of history and PSHE lessons.

❒ A multinational body formed after the First World War.

Choosing Suitable Headings and Subheadings

For this kind of question, you will be expected to choose a heading or subheading from a selection. This could be an overall heading for the entire piece, or possibly a subheading for a specific paragraph or portion of the text. Try to choose a heading/subheading which suits the text both in terms of tone and content.

Choose the most suitable heading for the entire text:

❒ War is Hell.

❒ Head teacher urges parents to teach their children about the war.

❒ School's focus on First World War is met with good reception.

❒ Remembering the Fallen.

Choose the most suitable subheading for paragraph 3:

❐ Why the First World War matters.

❐ Head teacher reminds us of the importance of the First World War.

❐ How the Nazis rose to power.

❐ A brief history of the 20th Century.

Judging Statements about the Text

This type of question will ask you to evaluate a selection of statements made about the text. You must decide if these statements are supported by the text, implicitly supported (implied), unsupported by the text, implicitly contradicted or explicitly contradicted.

Use the following abbreviations to evaluate the statements:

S   – is supported by the text.

I   – is implied by the text.

NE – is unsupported by the text (no evidence for it).

IC – is implicitly contradicted by the text.

EC – is explicitly contradicted by the text.

❐ The League of Nations was founded in 1920.

❐ The overall initiative was a success.

❐ The more sombre tone of the First World War inspired teachers to make light-hearted activities for students, such as roleplays.

❐ The assemblies were well received.

❐ Parents/guardians were frequently assisting in their child's education regarding 20th Century history.

Considering Readership and Target Audience

Questions following this format will expect you to identify the most suitable audience for the text. You will also need to highlight the least suitable audience for the text.

Use the following notation to show which audience is most suitable and which audience is least suitable:

MS – Most suitable.

LS – Least suitable.

☐ Government officials.

☐ Other head teachers/leadership teams in nearby schools.

☐ Parents/guardians of students in the school.

☐ Trainee teachers.

Comprehension – Answers and Explanations

In this section, you will find answers for the comprehension sample questions. Explanations have been included for each question, so that you can understand the reasoning used.

Presenting the Main Points of a Text

The main points of the text are as follows:

1. Parents/guardians should make their children aware of the First World War.

The reasoning for this is that the entire final paragraph is devoted to this point. It is also accompanied by one of the few quotes in the text, signifying its importance further. More importantly, the paragraph denotes this point as the final part of the initiative, which further suggests that it is one of the main points of the text.

2. The school has decided to create a larger focus on 20th Century history.

This is considered a main point because it is the aim of one of the main projects listed at the start of the text. The subject of the entire text revolves around this point.

3. Young students might not be exposed to the history of the war in a sensitive manner.

This is the focus of paragraph 4, and is one of the main points, because it is the motivation for both of the projects introduced in the first paragraph. Since the entire text is focused on these two projects, the reason for introducing them is an important point for the texts.

4. The First World War is one of the most important events in recent history.

This is a main point, because it is the subject of a major paragraph (paragraph 3) and includes a quote. It is also part of the head teacher's motivation for introducing the programme.

Other Points

When looking for the main points of a text, keep an eye out for the main initiatives, programmes or strategies referenced. Also make sure that your choices include points which are in the passage – it is possible that some of the choices are not actually explicit in the text.

Be sure to re-read each paragraph since main points tend to be the focus of at least one paragraph. It would be unusual for someone to write a text with a main point which only had one sentence devoted to it.

Once you've chosen what you believe to be the main points of the text, read them back to yourself and consider if they cover the majority of the text's material. If it helps, it might be worth imagining that you had to summarise this text to someone over the telephone. Would your choices include the essential things people need to know about the text?

In some cases, it may seem as though most (or perhaps even all) of the choices given could be main points. In this scenario, choose the points which seem to be the most important.

Matching the Content of the Text to a Summary

The most suitable summary for paragraphs 4 and 5 is:

3. The head teacher was concerned that students were not learning enough about the First World War outside of school. The new classes focus on it were received well.

This summary is most suitable since it encompasses the main points of the two paragraphs. The focus of paragraph 4 is on the head teacher's concern about students' understanding of the First World War, while paragraph 5 covers the success of these classes. Therefore, this summary is quite adequate.

The other summaries are less adequate because they either a) don't provide a summary of the paragraphs in question, or b) don't focus on the main points of the two paragraphs.

The first and last choices focus on the main points of other paragraphs. While they might suit those paragraphs, they do not provide a summary of paragraphs 4 and 5.

In comparison, the second choice contains content from paragraph 5, but not paragraph 4. Therefore, it is not an adequate summary. Even if it did include content from paragraph 4, it might still be considered insufficient since it does not focus on the key point of paragraph 5: that the new lessons were well-received.

Other Points

When trying to find a suitable summary, make sure it encompasses the key points of all the paragraphs you have been asked to find a summary for. The aim of a summary is to compile the most important points as briefly as possible. Shorter summaries may be preferable, but only if they cover everything they need to.

Highlighting the Meaning of Words and Phrases

The closest substitute for the given phrase is:

2. … And therefore compensated for the sombre tone…

This choice is most suitable because 'compensated' is a synonym for 'counter balanced'.

The other choices were unsuitable because they do not mean the same thing. The first choice uses the word 'reduced,' which suggests that the sombre tone of the First World War lessons was lessened by the light-hearted assemblies. However, this is not the case: these assemblies acted as a counterbalance. While they did not add to the sombre tone of the First World War (as the third choice suggests), they did not actively work against it either. Instead, these assemblies acted as some relief from the more serious tone of the lessons.

Likewise, the fourth choice uses the word 'overridden,' which implies that these assemblies outweighed the tone of the lessons. Again, this is not what the original phrase is saying. Rather than dominating the tone of the lessons, the assemblies acted as a counterbalance, which suggests that they are approximately equal. Therefore, the fourth choice is also unsuitable.

Other Points

This kind of question can be tricky, since it requires an understanding of what specific words mean. However, it's almost impossible to predict which words you need to know. If you are unsure of what the word means, look for the context in the sentence – sometimes you can figure out what the word means by how it's used.

In addition, be sure to re-read the paragraph the phrase belongs to, or even the wider text, since they might give a clue of what the word means. For example, if the phrase in the question used the word 'dismal' to describe something, and you weren't sure what the word meant, another part of the text may have another description of the same thing, which in turn might provide a hint.

Sequencing Information from the Text

The correct choices in order are:

2. Create a focus on the First World War in all History and PSHE lessons.

FIRST.

6. Devote assemblies to discussion about 20th Century history.

SECOND.

4. Encourage parents/guardians to teach their children about 20th Century history.

THIRD.

The other points are incorrect since they are not supported by the text (1, 3), or are not made explicit by it (5, 7). Generally speaking, the sequencing of information questions will require you to find points which are explicitly referred to, rather than have to make inferences about the information being sequenced.

Other Points

For this question, look for clues in the text which reveal the steps in the process. Generally speaking, the order of the steps will flow logically through the text – it's unlikely that the third step in the process will be listed first. Moreover, the text may denote the steps as "firstly…", "secondly…" and so on.

Also make sure that your choices only include steps which are found in the text. It's possible that some of the choices will not be points in the text, and therefore they cannot be suitable answers for this question.

Completing a List based on the Content of the Text

To finish the list, you must choose the following:

6. Encourage more students to study History.

3. Increase awareness for different kinds of depiction about the war.

5. Be an example to other schools.

The answers above are worded slightly differently to how they appear in the main text. This could be the case in the test, and therefore you must be able to match the paraphrased answers with the bullet points in the text. Therefore, make sure you re-read the list of bullet points in order to identify the correct phrasings.

The other choices were incorrect because they didn't include information from the list. You should only choose answers which contain content from the list.

Other Points

For this kind of question, you only need to focus on the list featured in the text – you can ignore the other content for the time being. However, make sure you have read the entire text at least once before attempting this question, since it can provide some context for the list, making it easier to spot the correct paraphrased answers.

Attributing Statements to Elements of the Text

The correct answers are as follows:

The League of Nations	A multinational body formed after the First World War.
The 20th Century Awareness Project	A project with the aim of changing the school's overall focus regarding history.
The First World War Awareness Programme	A project devoted to changing the focus of History and PSHE lessons.
PSHE	Personal Social Health Education.

Other Points

For this kind of question, read the entire text in order to find statements which match the elements given. These elements are usually categories of some kind such as groups of people (e.g. qualified teachers, trainee teachers) or projects or programmes such as those given in the sample question.

Choosing Suitable Headings and Subheadings

The most suitable heading for the entire test is:

3. School's focus on First World War is met with good reception.

This heading is the most suitable since it adequately explains the main point of the text (that the school has placed more emphasis on the First World War) and the major result of it (it is well-received). Moreover, since the text is from a fictional teaching journal, it needs a shorter title to remain interesting. Therefore, option 2 is unsuitable.

The first and fourth options are also unsuitable, since they are too dramatic, and do not match the message of the text. Option 1 bears little relevance to the text, and while option 4 is slightly more relevant, it doesn't outline the content of the text.

The most suitable subheading for paragraph 3 is:

1. Why the First World War matters.

Again, this subheading is most suitable since it is shorter than option 2, and adequately introduces the main point of the paragraph. The third option does not represent the message of the paragraph, since it isn't focused on the Nazi party's rise to power, and option 4 is far too vague.

Other Points

For questions of this kind, keep an eye out for the target audience. The text may be introduced as a journal article, a government document, or possibly even a school newsletter. The kind of text will contribute to what kind of heading or subheading is most suitable. Government documents may use more technical jargon, while newsletters will opt for a shorter title with simpler words to be more effective.

Regardless of the text's source, relevant titles are always preferable to overdramatic, irrelevant ones.

Judging Statements about the Text

The correct answers for this sample question are:

The League of Nations was founded in 1920. – S

The overall initiative was a success. – NE

The more sombre tone of the First World War inspired teachers to make light-hearted activities for students, such as roleplays. – I

The assemblies were well received. – EC

Parents/guardians were frequently assisting in their child's education regarding 20th Century history. - IC

- *"The League of Nations was founded in 1920."* This is supported by the text since it is explicit in paragraph 3.

- *"The overall initiative was a success."* This is not supported or contradicted by the text. We know from the text that the classes were well-received and the assemblies were poorly received, but we cannot tell if the goals of the initiative listed at the end of the text were met. Therefore, there is no evidence in the text that supports this statement.

- *"The more sombre tone of the First World War inspired teachers to make light-hearted activities for students, such as roleplays."* While not made explicit in the text, we can make this inference since it is mentioned that the First World War lessons had a sombre tone in paragraph 6. We also know that teachers introduced roleplays from paragraph 5, and therefore we can infer that these were used to keep the classes light-hearted in tone.

- *"The assemblies were well received."* This is explicitly contradicted by the text, as we can see from paragraph 6.

- *"Parents/guardians were frequently assisting in their child's education regarding 20th Century history."* This is implicitly contradicted by the text, since the head teacher is urging parents/guardians to help in making their children more aware of 20th Century events.

Other Points

This kind of question may be one of the most demanding of the whole section, since it requires you to read the entire text very closely. More importantly, you need to be clear on what the different attributes mean.

Supported by the text:

This simply means that the text provides explicit evidence for the statement. If the text says that the League of Nations was founded in 1920, and one of the statements says the same thing, then the statement is supported by the text.

Implied by the text:

The text gives implicit evidence for the statement. Unlike statements supported by the text, this means that the statement is supported but it isn't entirely clear. For this, you may need to "read between the lines" in order to figure out what statements that the text implicitly supports.

For example, if the text stated that older students were more receptive to the lessons than younger students, the implication would be that the younger students didn't particularly enjoy the First World War lessons.

Unsupported by the text (no evidence):

This means that the text offers no evidence to support the statement, and also offers no evidence to contradict or refute the statement. Simply put, there is no way to confirm whether the statement is true or false based purely on the information in the text.

Explicitly contradicted by the text:

The statement is directly refuted by information in the text. If the text says that the assemblies were poorly received, and the statement says that the assemblies were well-received, then there is a contradiction. Since this contradiction is clear or explicit, then the statement is explicitly contradicted by the test.

It may help to think of this as the opposite of "supported by the text," which means that the statement is clearly supported by the information in the text. In this case, the information in the text clearly opposes the statement.

Implicitly contradicted by the text:

Similar to the explicit contradiction, this means that the statement is contradicted by the text, although it might not be clear. For example, if the text shows the head teacher urging parents to assist in making their children more aware of 20th Century history, then the implication is that parents are currently not doing so. So, if the statement claims that parents are helping, then there is an implicit contradiction.

In a sense, this is the opposite of "implied by the text," but in this case the text implicitly opposes the statement rather than implicitly supports it.

Considering Readership and Target Audience

The most and least suitable target audiences are:

MS – Other head teachers/leadership teams in nearby schools.

LS – Trainee teachers.

Since the text is an article from an education journal, it is most suitable for teachers who have an interest in the wider teaching community. Moreover, since the school is trying to set an example for other schools (as mentioned in the list), it makes most sense for other leadership teams to be the target readership for the article.

Trainee teachers are the least suitable since, while the article may be interesting for them to read, it won't have as much of an effect on them as parents and guardians in the school community who want to know about the current events of the school. Likewise, government officials are a slightly more suitable target audience, since the programme could be brought into the national curriculum if successful.

Other Points

Target audience can be determined by a number of factors. Firstly, large amounts of jargon might suggest that the audience is for specialists such as government officials. Simpler vocabulary might suggest a target audience of younger or less specialised people, such as parents or perhaps trainee teachers.

Secondly, the introduction of the text may give a hint as to what the intended readership is. The text used in this section is from a fictional education journal, which suggests that the target audience is intended to be teachers rather than parents. If the source came from a school newsletter, then it's likely written with parents in mind.

Finally, make note of the content of the text overall when determining target audience. Who is the content relevant to? The text would not be useful for students within the school, since they are already experiencing the new programmes and therefore do not need an article to tell them about it.

Job Suitability Tests

Police Suitability Tests are used in an early stage of Police recruitment processes to allow recruiting cops to get a sense of the applicants' general strengths and potential weaknesses. It achieves this by presenting a series of statements about work-related behaviour. The applicant is then asked to decide the extent to which they agree with these statements, out of options such 'Completely Disagree' through to 'Completely Agree'.

For example, questions could include things like "I always follow through on commitments I have made', 'I always put maximum effort into tasks I am set'. As you can see, the statements are fairly simplistic, and usually you can tell what recruiters would want to hear. But, it is very important that you answer these questions honestly, in order to impart an accurate representation of yourself. This is not only important for recruiters, who will of course ascertain your suitability sooner or later, but for yourself, as the questions can allow you to consider whether you are right for a role with the Police, and whether you really want it.

Below you will find a selection of sample questions of this nature, which do not have 'correct' or 'incorrect' answers. In any case, fill out the table by putting a tick in the most suitable box for each statement. Use them to get a sense of how your honest responses might go down with recruiters!

Statement	Completely disagree	Strongly disagree	Somewhat disagree	Neither agree nor disagree	Somewhat agree	Strongly agree	Completely agree
I always follow through on commitments I have made.							
I always put maximum effort into tasks I am set.							
I always call out injustice when I see it.							
Being honest at all times is important to me.							
I treat everyone fairly, regardless of background.							

Audio Tests

Audio tests are designed to test how well applicants can retain and deal with information that they have listened to. This is of course, an extremely important skill for a member of the Police. Good listening skills will come into play on a daily basis for a cop, who will have to listen to instructions from their superiors, relay information to those under them, as well as interact and be sensitive to members of the public.

Follow the link below for a blog containing sample Audio Tests:

https://www.how2become.com/blog/civil-enforcement-officer-listening-test/

(Note: the blog contains Civil Enforcement Officer Listening Tests used in the UK. However, we believe they will still be extremely helpful for preparing for an Australian Police Audio Tests – they assess the same skills and allow for practice).

Closing Comments

You have now reached the end of the guide and no doubt will be ready to start preparing for an Australian Police Agency recruitment process. The majority of candidates who pass the selection process have a number of common attributes.

1. They believe in themselves.

The first factor is self-belief. Regardless of what anyone tells you, you can become a Police Officer. Just like any job of this nature, you have to be prepared to work hard in order to be successful. Make sure that you have the self-belief to pass the selection process and fill your mind with positive thoughts.

2. They prepare fully.

The second factor is preparation. Those people who achieve in life prepare fully for every eventuality and that is what you must do when you apply to become a Police Officer. Work very hard and especially concentrate on your weak areas.

3. They persevere.

Perseverance is a fantastic word. Everybody comes across obstacles or setbacks in their life, but it is what you do about those setbacks that is important. If you fail at something, then consider *'why'* you have failed. This will allow you to improve for next time and if you keep improving and trying, success will eventually follow. Apply this same method of thinking when you apply to join a Police Agency.

4. They are self-motivated.

How much do you want this job? Do you want it, or do you really want it? When you apply to join the Police, you should want it more than anything in the world. Your levels of self-motivation will shine through on your application and during your interview. For the weeks and months leading up to the selection process, try to stay as motivated as you can, and always keep your fitness levels up.

Work hard, stay focused and you can achieve anything that you set your mind to!

For more help with becoming a Police Officer see our other guide:

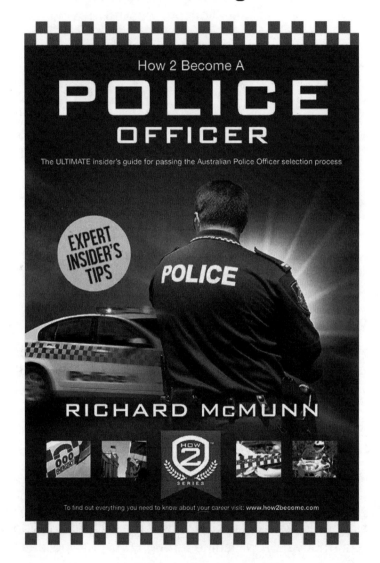

www.HOW2BECOME.com